Where Animals Help People

Best Always

Dr. Jim Marshall

2-7-05

Where Animals Help People

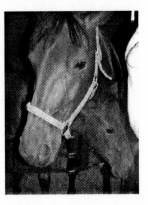

✦

Surviving Suicidal Depression

An Autobiography by James O. Marshall, DVM

iUniverse, Inc.
New York Lincoln Shanghai

Where Animals Help People
Surviving Suicidal Depression

iUniverse, Inc.

For information address:
iUniverse, Inc.
2021 Pine Lake Road, Suite 100
Lincoln, NE 68512
www.iuniverse.com

ISBN: 0-595-31971-8 (pbk)
ISBN: 0-595-66452-0 (cloth)

Printed in the United States of America

This book is dedicated to my wife, Ruthie, and our four children, Otey, Cynthia, Peter, and Jennifer; the treasures of my life.

You will soon learn how Ruth proved to be a pillar of strength supporting a sick husband while raising four wonderful children.

Contents

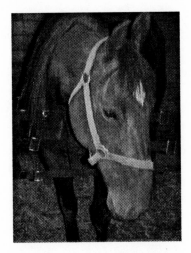

Acknowledgments

I am indebted to several people who helped make this book a reality:

- Chuck Elliott, MD and his wife Kathy, a family therapist—for writing the introduction to this book and supporting my decision to form the Foundation and write this book.

- Margherita Martinez—my very efficient assistant who typed every word onto a computer disk for publishing. Most of this was a struggle; understanding my scribbling on a legal pad and making it sound okay.

- Valerie Roehme—my former secretary at the Fayetteville Veterinary Hospital, who typed up the first part of the book.

- Gail Foreman—a good friend who shared her expertise in the organization and publishing of the manuscript, and who gave her constant encouragement to *finish the book*!!!

- Bonita Voiland—Assistant Dean and Professor Emeritus F.H. Fox at the NYS Veterinary College for their suggestions.

- Mark Rapp, MD, Mike Lynch, Hannah Davis, and Dolores Card—medical professionals who provided their opinions and their time reviewing the manuscript.

- Bill and Shirley Molesky for their support. Shirley has been a major benefactor of animal welfare in Central New York for years. Her son, Bill, is a professional consultant for many publishers, and proof read this book as a personal favor.

- Jack Hodgson—a friend and experienced author, (pen name Jonathan Hyde), who gave his advice and help in publishing this book.

Introduction

This book is about courage and determination. It is also about love and humor. It tells the story of a man who lived with depressive illness for 23 years, survived two suicide attempts, and who now wants to be a resource for those who are suffering from the same infirmity.

Doctor Marshall reveals himself in a very humble way, telling his readers about his battle with depressive illness in a very endearing manner.

Being friends with Jim and Ruth during this difficult time we shared their struggle and are very aware of the pain they both endured.

Now that Dr. Marshall has come through the dark tunnel he is dedicating his life to help others know that there is hope for those coping with depression.

We know you will appreciate the poignant telling of this memoir citing his struggle and his determination to give back through the Jim Marshall Farms Foundation.

Dr. Charles and Kathleen Elliott

A Special Message from
the Author

Why would a happily married fifty-two-year old professional man who had achieved the American Dream put a .357 Magnum revolver to his head and pull the trigger on Friday, the thirteenth of December, 1985?

I have been writing this story not just for your entertainment, but to educate and motivate you.

The lesson to be learned is that depressive illness is not a personal weakness. It is a deadly disease that is sometimes fatal and affects million of individuals. There are no vaccines to prevent it, and complete recovery may take years if at all. No one is immune from its grasp.

The motivation I am hoping you receive is to get involved in helping yourself and others in finding a cure for this disease.

Once you have embarked on this journey to help others, you will have found the secret to living a happy, fulfilled life.

When you help someone—you help yourself.

James O. Marshall, DVM
May 28, 2004

Prologue

Depression touches the lives of most people. Minor periods of the *blues* affect everyone. More serious and long standing periods of depression affect millions. Some get treatment and recover. Many more go unrecognized—seriously impairing their productivity and happiness. I believe it can be a major factor in a family break-up, including divorce.

Depression is one of the leading causes of death—often a person is completely healthy in every way but so despondent that he or she chooses death over life and attempts suicide. I was one of the many who have attempted to end their lives (not once, but twice)—and one of the few lucky ones that were unsuccessful and survived! I hope my story helps others to understand this illness as it affects themselves, family members, and friends or people that they know who are suffering. It may even save someone's happiness, job, marriage, or even their life.

Jim Marshall Farms is a special place I have created *where animals help people*, especially depressed people, who have lost the meaning and the incredible wonderful value of the *gift of life*. Having spent a lifetime in the greatest profession—Veterinary Medicine—I have had the benefit first hand of witnessing the beneficial bond between animals and mankind. If you let them, animals can add love and meaning to your life. Some find it in a cat, dog, horse, cow, sheep, pig, bird, raccoon, lizard, or other exotic species. My favorites are cats, dogs, and especially horses. Winston Churchill said that *"The outside of a horse is good for the inside of a man/woman."* I believe it, and at Jim Marshall Farms, you will find lots of horses. Actually, it is just one farm, but I used the plural because I hope someday other communities can have a Jim Marshall Farm—*where animals help people*.

I battled depression for over twenty-three years of my life, some periods worse than others. I have spent thousands and thousands of dollars, seen more than a dozen psychiatrists and psychologists, taken more than twenty-five different drugs, and spent time in several mental hospitals. Since the year 2000, I feel I have completely recovered and love life more than ever. Now I want to tell my story. I hope you like the book, understand depression better, and visit a Jim Marshall Farm someday. I want you to help yourself or anyone you know suffer-

1

ing from this dreadful illness. It can be devastating to one's happiness, and in some cases, even fatal.

The brain is the most complex organ in our body, consisting of over one billion cells. Our goal is to have all of these cells function perfectly, maximizing our potential and happiness. However, many of us will experience breakdowns in our mental health. Restoring one-hundred percent of the proper function of all these cells is a challenge almost everyone faces at some point in their lives.

There is a crying need for improvement in mental health therapy. If we can put a man on the moon, we can certainly do a better job with mental health. Pursuing this goal is the number one commitment for the rest of my life.

Suicide, due to depressive illness claims the lives of thirty thousand of our U.S. citizens that are reported each year. There are probably an equal number of suicides that are attributed to other accidental causes to avoid embarrassment to their families. In my seventy years of life I have known several wonderful friends, including a relative, who have terminated their lives as a result of this illness. It is the memory of these tragic deaths, together with my own miraculous survival that has motivated me to write this book. If my story can convince one person to resist suicide and eventually restore their happiness as I have, I will be well rewarded for my efforts.

1

Born on the Farm

There I am in 1935, the little boy on the right sitting on the stairs.

Three things in our lives we have no control over: who our parents are and where and how we grow up. I was lucky on all three counts. My heritage was great: both of my parents were from farm families that went back several generations in agriculture. I was born and grew up on a farm just south of Munnsville, New York, twenty-five miles southeast of Syracuse. I was the fourth of five children, arriving less than a year after my older sister, Zoe Mary, making Zoe and me *"Irish Twins."* My birthplace was my parents' bedroom in the farmhouse, and the doctor's fee was fifteen dollars. I often tell the story that my father took one look at me and complained that the fee was too high which was not really true. The date was November 4, 1933. As fate would have it, fifty-two years and thirty-nine days later on Friday the thirteenth of December 1985, I would spend the night in the same bedroom with a .357 Magnum, planning to end my suffering with one shot to the head. The gun went off and miraculously I survived. God definitely had a plan for my survival, and the remainder of my life.

Growing up on a dairy farm, working together in a farm family is truly the greatest way to start a life. We all developed tremendous values of ambition, faith, patience, perseverance, and loyalty that would guarantee our success in later life. Working with animals was a joy, and this eventually led me to the wonderful profession of Veterinary Medicine.

We had all sorts of animals on our farm: six mules, two workhorses, a pony, always a larger riding horse, about one hundred Holstein cattle, and over a thousand white leghorn chickens. One thing was for certain: if you grow up on a farm, you learn how to work hard from dawn to dusk. At 4:30 a.m., even before daylight the cows had to be milked. Breakfast was at 7:30, and then we went off to school at Stockbridge Valley Central. After school there were always farm chores and the night milking, which finished up at about 7:00 p.m. when we all congregated in the farmhouse for the evening meal. After supper, almost all the men and boys would fall asleep reading the newspaper, while my mom and sisters did the dishes.

I recall the evening when my sister, Zoe, brought home my future brother-in-law to meet the family. After supper they turned down the lights to show us all some slides. When they finished and turned up the lights, the entire audience was sound asleep, even my mother. One thing farmers do not need after a day's work, a big meal, and a warm house is a sleeping pill. Many years later as I suffered from major depression, I could not sleep, which was agony! Even to this day, with depression behind me, I have the same habit of falling asleep early, but now I fall asleep watching TV.

The teachers rarely gave us homework because nearly everyone lived on a farm and there was no time for it at home. Still we did well on the NYS Regents tests. I remember I received a perfect one hundred on the eighth grade math Regents, one of the very few in the state. My Aunt Ruth was the math teacher that year, and she was truly proud of her nephew student. We also were blessed with terrific grandparents, aunts, and uncles. My mother's parents were devout Methodists, never missing church. They both lived to the age of ninety-five and I doubt that a drop of alcohol ever touched their lips, which I can attest was not true with their grandchildren.

The first available photo of the future James O. Marshall, DVM

When we were real young, our grandparents would pick us up and take us to camp for a night or two. They had a 1929 Roadster we all called the "Bump-bump car." The camp was on the backside of our family farm overlooking Stockbridge Falls, which is a very beautiful and special spot that holds very special and fond memories for all of us kids. There was no electricity and no plumbing. We used a two-holer outhouse and went to a nearby spring for water. I still remember the morning breakfast Grandma Lyman would make—pancakes with real maple syrup and brown sugar. We had several family get-togethers there and I can still remember waiting that endless sixty minutes after eating before we could go swimming in the falls. My nephew, Skosh, recently had his marriage ceremony at the falls. Although he is blind, the falls are a special place for him also, because he loves the sounds of the water.

Time with my father's parents was also special. Grandfather Marshall was a prominent gentleman farmer, vice president of the Oneida Valley National Bank, and a shrewd investor. I remember him sitting on the back porch, smoking his pipe, and watching the farm operation. One day, at the age of seven, I was driving a team of horses back to the horse barn. I was slapping the reins up and down at the time. He jumped off the porch and admonished me to hold the reins steady. Sixty years later I'm still driving horses and I remember to hold the reins steady. Grandmother Marshall, on the other hand, was a workaholic. Before I was born the farm raised hops, and at harvest time she would care for the bedding and meals for up to thirty-five Native American migrant workers who would stay at the farm and pick the hops. She would start at two in the morning and had only one woman to help her. How many gals in this day and age could cook three meals a day for thirty-five people for two weeks?

I remember she would always call me James and every morning when staying with them she would ask me, "*Did you put on a clean wrapper (underwear), James?*" We always went to her house for Thanksgiving and Christmas, and the spread she put on was fantastic. We always started with oyster stew, which is a Marshall family tradition, and there was no end to the pies (always with cheese), cookies, and candy, as well as the turkey at Thanksgiving and ham at Christmas. Grandfather would never sit down to a table with thirteen, so we always had to work around that superstition by setting an extra table. Grandfather also chewed tobacco and there were several spittoons around the house for grandmother to clean. How many of our wives would put up with that today? She died from lung cancer. She never smoked in her life, but she did have a lifetime of inhaling the smoke from grandfather's pipe.

My favorite uncle was definitely Uncle Fred. He was a bachelor and lived with my Grandmother Marshall after Grampa died. He inherited the homestead and I spent many, many good times working with him.

After my grandmother died, he was very lonely living alone in the large house, so my mom and dad invited him to live with them in *Stone Manor* where they had plenty of room. In later years, Uncle Fred would live with us and helped me in building my veterinary hospital. He was invaluable! One day a labor inspector stopped and spotted Uncle Fred digging a ditch. He also noticed a guard missing from the cement mixer. When the inspector tracked me down, I said, "*Show me!*" When we returned to the mixer, Uncle Fred had the guard back in place. He did write up a summons for not having a Workman's Compensation policy to cover Uncle Fred. It was a shock to find out that here in America you could not have an uncle help you out (no salary) without a Workman's Compensation policy!

My older brother Fred moved into the Marshall homestead and took over the farm from Uncle Fred. What we didn't know was that a brain tumor was growing slowly in my brother that would ravage his life. I, too, in later life would discover a brain tumor that brought on depression. The incidence is supposed to be one in ten thousand, so it's real bad luck for brothers to both have brain tumors. Both of us suffered greatly. I survived, but Fred did not.

Mother was a special person who devoted one-hundred percent of her time and energy to her family. She raised five children, took care of over a thousand chickens, cooked three meals a day for us, plus a couple of hired men who lived in our house, and she kept the house spic and span. I can remember one hired man who would get drunk on weekends, come home, and wet the bed. She had this to clean up on Monday morning. During harvest time, she would cook the noontime meal for up to twenty workers. Our food was not from the supermarket, but from the basement where we had canned goods, a potato bin, crocks of sauerkraut, salt pork, smoked ham, and a huge freezer (one of the first in the area). All this came from the farm itself. We had a large garden that produced all the potatoes and vegetables that were canned and frozen. The pork, beef, and poultry were all raised on the farm.

Killing the animals brings back vivid memories. Chickens were slaughtered by chopping the heads off. They would jump and flutter for several minutes, leaving a bloody mess before they died. The pigs were rolled over on their backs, their throats were cut with a huge knife, and they walked around until they died. The steers were shot right between the eyes and died immediately. A man would come to the farm to help with the slaughter, cutting up the meat for the freezer. Father had a huge cast-iron kettle to heat up boiling water to dip the pigs and chickens into so we could scrape off all the hair from the pigs and feathers from the chickens. I remember the pig bladders were blown up with air, tied off, and given to us kids as a ball to play with. They were good for a few days, until they started to smell. After a slaughter session, we would eat liver three times a day for a week or two until it was all used up, because liver had to be eaten fresh. My brother Fred hated liver and gagged. We always had to clean up our plates no matter what was served. I think I'm the only one in the family who still likes liver.

After my younger brother, Tom, was born, mother developed rheumatoid arthritis that would leave her in pain the rest of her life. Her knees gave out, but they couldn't do the knee replacements yet. She suffered and suffered but never complained. Depression, or the potential for depression, is inherited and it was definitely in Mom's family. I sometimes wonder if it was a factor in lowering her immunity, allowing the rheumatoid arthritis to devastate her life. None of us kids seemed to be affected by depression at a very young age, with the exception of my older brother Fred. He would get into some very foul moods and stay in his room for hours. I remember one day the mowing machine he was operating broke down. He just left it in the field, went to his room, and stayed there refusing to come out or talk to anyone. My parents were at a loss as to what to do, but he would eventually come out of it. Mother passed away at home, and hugging her dead body was the most painful memory of my life. Her suffering was over and she had entered a better, pain-free life, which we all wanted for her.

My father, Otis Potter Marshall, was an amazing man. Growing up, I always took his great potential for granted. I thought everyone's dad was alike. Only upon reaching adulthood did I start to realize what a dynamic man he really was. The youngest of three sons, he was born just across the creek from where my mother was born. They both were born and grew up on farms that were separated by Oneida Creek. Father did well in school and planned to attend Cornell University, as did his older brother Frank. He went down to Ithaca on the morning train with his entire luggage. After lugging the bags around campus for several hours, he decided that college was not for him, returning home on the night train.

Since his older brother Frank had bought his own farm, my father soon followed with the purchase of a farm south of Munnsville on the Pratts Hollow Road. This is where I was born and grew up. The farm was mainly a dairy farm, but my dad was always looking for ways to make a buck. Before I was born, he cut ice from a farm pond, packed it in an old barn with sawdust and sold it well into the summer. The winters in Central New York were brutal back in those days, and several cuttings of ice were taken from the pond every winter. Father took a liking to mules, and I can remember as many as three teams of mules and one team of horses at a time. My special job every summer was raking hay scatterings with a Jenny mule (female mule) and a dump rake. Mules weren't the easiest to drive. They are very hardy and very stubborn, but they would out-work a horse any day of the week. A mule would never go near a woodchuck hole where it could break a leg and would never drink water when hot like a horse would causing colic and founder. I can never remember any of our mules getting sick. The Old Erie Canal, which crossed New York State, passes north of our farm, and the barges were always pulled with teams of mules. Driving that mule initiated a love of the equine species that would continue the rest of my life.

Our first pony on the farm was *Calico*. When she arrived, we all wanted to ride her right away. After a few beers, a hired hand, Seymour Bristol, would put us up on the saddle, hand us the reins, and tell us to hang on. He then took a broom and whacked her across the butt. We took off at a dead gallop and I can't remember any of us kids falling off. All of us learned to ride, but I don't recommend this method of starting out to anyone else. Over the years, other riding horses came along—*Mabel, Major,* and *Brownie*. My brother Fred was riding *Mabel* one day when she took off at a gallop for the barn. When she ran into the barn, he was knocked off her back with the low ceiling. Many of us think that this injury caused a brain tumor to start growing on his frontal lobe. This tumor grew to the size of a small grapefruit before it was diagnosed and removed, devastating his life. *Major* was very classy and was by far my favorite horse. If you pulled back on the reins, he would stand perfectly straight up on his hind legs, just like *Silver* would do for the Lone Ranger.

In 1943, *Farm Life*, a country magazine, came to our farm to do an article on our family. I was nine years old at the time and was photographed wearing a big straw hat and driving an old farm truck with no door. This was a wonderful article showing pictures of our happy family working together on the farm. Few youngsters today have the opportunity to spend time on a farm and mingle with the many farm animals. This experience has led me to develop *Jim Marshall Farms*, a farm facility *where animals help people*. Believe me, it can be very effective therapy for both the very young and very old alike. No one would believe that this happy nine-year-old farm boy would attempt to end his life forty-three years later.

Father hired the Ward boys on occasion to help out on the farm. They became celebrities years later when Delbert Ward put his older brother Bill, who was suffering from a terminal illness, out of his misery by suffocating him with a pillow. The murder trial received a great deal of publicity and Delbert was acquitted. Later they were featured in a movie, *My Brother's Keeper*, which became very popular. The four Ward brothers lived together after their mother died: Roscoe, Bill, Lyman, and Delbert. I remember two occasions working with the boys. One was with Lyman stacking hay in the barn together off an elevator. Every time he would place a bale in an opening where it would just fit, he would look at me and exclaim: "*A baby's born!*" This would go on all day long. The other memory was with Roscoe. Father was working us real hard one morning and Roscoe was starting to fade. He ate enough for three men at lunch, which my mother always made for the workers. After lunch, Roscoe disappeared into the cornfield and was never seen again that day. None of them had a license, so they would be seen every week, all four on a tractor going to town for groceries. It's hard to believe today that from all the people living in the Stockbridge Valley, the Ward boys would become the celebrities.

Father was the first in the valley to own pick-up balers, which would bale hay right in the fields. They were huge cumbersome machines with an automatic wiring device placing wires around the bales which weighed over one-hundred pounds. The balers required one man to drive the tractor and another to tie the wires around the bales. That was my job and it was a dusty, dirty place to work. Father charged twenty-five cents a bale and it was our goal to bale four hundred bales a day. This meant an income of one-hundred dollars a day, and in those days was a fortune for one day's work. Father was mighty proud of me when I would return at night filthy dirty, but with a report of baling four-hundred bales that day.

One Fourth of July we had to bale hay in a stony field. The baler slid off a rock and crushed my foot under the heavy baler. I was laid up with a big cast on my leg, unable to do much on the farm. During this time, Leon Pratt, the 4-H agent for Madison County, stopped and asked me if I would join the county team at the New York State poultry judging contest held at the State Fair in September. I went through the contest and on to the midway for some fun. Soon an announcement came over the PA system that I was to return to the poultry building. There, I found out my score was the best out of one-hundred contestants.

This meant that I was on the New York State team, which was slated to go to the Boston Gardens for the national contest—my first trip to the Big City. Full of excitement, we were motoring into Boston with Professor Ogle from Cornell, plus the other 4-H team members. As we approached the city, suddenly a trooper car pulled us over and stopped in front of the car. A trooper jumped out of the car with a machine gun trained on our car. Another trooper car pulled up behind us with another trooper training a machine gun on us from the rear. We were forced to get out of the car with our hands over our heads while we were frisked.

What we didn't know was that the famous *Brinks robbery* had just taken place and we were in an area of high suspicion. They thought they had the robbers! Finally, they let us go. Ever since that day, I've liked the farm better than the city.

Harvest time on the farm brings back fond memories of working together. We started driving trucks and tractors at about seven years of age, and by the age of nine and ten, we were pretty proficient at operating farm machinery. We rotated between our farm and my two uncles' farms for threshing and silo filling. Working together with relatives on the farm, helping each other, creates family bonds that last a lifetime. This is clearly missing in today's independent living.

There were also some sad memories of growing up on the farm. One of the worst was the time over a hundred baby chicks died because I made a mistake in adjusting the brooder temperature. The brooder temperature has to be perfect when the chicks are first born. If it's too cold, they will bunch together to stay warm and some will be suffocated. When it's too hot, their little lungs are cooked and they die. With tears streaming down my face, I buried all the chicks in a grave. Later in my professional life, I caused the death of a horse when I mistakenly placed a stomach tube down the trachea instead of the esophagus, causing pneumonia and death. I was covered by insurance, but the guilt and pain were enormous. This sensitivity followed me through life and I could never shoot a deer or another animal.

Father was truly an entrepreneur. He not only bought the farm next door, but also six other farms that were owned by a wealthy lawyer who died. Some of the farms we fixed up and kept. The rest he sold. He was very successful and we all learned to work hard, keeping up with his expansion. Father was well liked and known throughout Central New York as Otey. He belonged to Rotary in Oneida for over twenty years, and was very popular with the businessmen in the big city of Oneida. Some of the natives were jealous and would say OPM stood for *Other People's Money*. Later in life, in addition to the farms, he started a fuel business and a tire business that my nephews still carry on. Well into his seventies, he would go out in the middle of the night to deliver fuel oil to customers, many of which would never pay him! He was also a board member at Morrisville Agricultural & Technology College, where he was instrumental in obtaining state funds for the school development. Later, they dedicated a building in his honor—*Marshall Hall*. In 1976, we had a huge family float for his eightieth birthday and the two-hundred-year celebration in town—two hundred for the USA and eighty for OPM. It was his last hurrah. He died following a stroke less than a year later. The whole area mourned his death and his funeral was huge! His death could possibly have been a factor in the onset of my depression in 1977.

The best advice he gave me as a young man starting out: "*Jim, you have to get up early and work hard all day, or you'll scratch a poor man's ass all your life.*"

My first talk in the *Big City* of Oneida in 1947. A 4-H demonstration on *Cooling Eggs*.

MARSHALL, JAMES
Salutatorian
President
College Entrance

Basketball, 4 yrs.; Baseball,
3 yrs.; Football, 3 yrs.;
Student Council Play, 2 yrs.;
Language Key, '50; Class Pres.
'47-48, '48-49, '49-50, '50-51;
Prize Speaking Trophy; Band, 4
yrs.; Silver Typing Key; Co-Bus.
Manager of Annual; 4-H, 6 yrs.

James O. Marshall #20 on the Varsity Basketball Team

James O. Marshall #7 on the Varsity Football Team

School and especially high school were the happiest times of my life. I was always successful and often had all A's on my report card. Mother would praise me, but Father was tough to please and would admonish me to try for all A+'s. I was very athletic and played on every possible team. There were only three—baseball, basketball, and a six-man football team. Basketball was my best sport, and I was a master of the two-hand set shot. In one game, I made twelve straight shots for twenty-four points—the highlight of my high school career. The present day three-point shot from nineteen feet would have been my cup of tea. Our school was so small that we had to play six-man football instead of eleven. Several schools in Central New York were in the same boat, so we had plenty of competition. The field was eighty yards long and a first down was fifteen yards. There were three linemen, a quarterback, and two running backs. I played left end, both offense and defense, and I liked defense best. In one game against the Rome School for the Deaf and Dumb, I deciphered the sign language for a pitch out to the halfback on my side. The next time they called the play I was there for the pitch-out and ran for a touchdown. However, my glory days as a high school star athlete ended when I went to Cornell. Attending a small high school in the country had its advantages. There were sixteen in my graduating class, and I was president of the freshman, sophomore, junior, and senior classes—*a big fish in a little pond!* Other highlights were playing in the band and public speaking. My senior year, I won the league public-speaking contest, and also gave Lincoln's Gettysburg Address at the Memorial Day ceremonies at Stockbridge Park.

Unfortunately, my driving record in my younger days was not too good. I wrecked two cars. Father liked Hudsons and we grew up driving Hudsons. My first accident happened when we went up to the Adirondacks for a weekend with friends, all in our teens. After taking our dates home, the front wheel of the car caught the soft shoulder of the road and rolled over several times down a steep embankment. Fortunately, no one was hurt. My father was against my trip saying, "You'll probably wreck the car." He proved to be correct and it was a quiet, painful trip with my father when we returned to the area to pick up the wreck. The second accident, also while I was driving a Hudson, happened when I was home from college one summer working for a Veterinarian nearby. I was taking my sister's dog in for a bath and the dog started eating my lunch on the front seat. When I tried to throw the dog into the back seat, I lost control of the car, hitting a tree. This drove the ignition key into my knee, which later required an operation to remove a bone chip. Another time I fell asleep coming home from

Cornell, driving into a deep ditch. Fortunately, all these accidents resulted in few injuries. I've been accident-free ever since.

Those early days were great. I was successful and having fun. No one would ever believe that later in life depression would consume my energy and I would become despondent and suicidal. No one is ever home free in this life, and I was destined to find that out.

2

Off To Cornell

It was taken for granted that I would go to college. Although Father only spent one day in college, he insisted that all of us kids go to college. My two older sisters (Ada May and Zoe Mary) and my older brother (Fred) had already started. I applied and was accepted at the Forestry College at Syracuse University and the Agricultural School at Cornell. Since my heritage for several generations was in agriculture, I opted for the College of Agriculture at Cornell.

Going from a graduating class of sixteen to Cornell University was a shocker. Now I was a *tiny little fish in a big, big pond.* My college life started in Dorm Two, which was an old Army barracks below the libe slope. I remember the first dorm meeting where we were told that only one out of three would survive to graduate. This was an eye-opener because I had assumed that everyone went to college and graduated. The temptation of booze, parties and girls was ever present. My first roommate succumbed in less than three months. I felt so bad for his mother, who was a wonderful person and worked so hard to send her fat, lazy son to Cornell. He would cut classes to play pool (for money) at the local saloons. Witnessing his mother's disappointment helped me vow that I would never do this to my parents. I buckled down and never failed a subject. I did have fun on the *Dorm Two* basketball team. Dick Schaap played on that team and later became a famous sportscaster. Meeting and making friends came easily and soon I was enjoying college life. I pledged the SAE fraternity and this fellowship was great. We were known on campus as the *Sleep and Eats* or *Sex above Everything.* My parents weren't too impressed with these descriptions, but I did keep my grades up so all was well.

Forty years later, one of my SAE fraternity brothers, Ed Feldman, contracted terminal cancer. One of his last wishes was to see his SAE pledge class brothers once more. He contacted all of us and organized a reunion at the fraternity house in June of 1995. Most of us had not seen each other for forty years. Lee Fingar, one of my best friends and roommate, still looked the same. Apparently I had changed and I suddenly realized that he didn't have a clue who I was. I went up to him and asked to borrow fifty cents for coffee since I was broke. He took one look at me, reached in his pocket and gave me fifty cents. I finally had to tell him who I was. The forty years, plus too much good food, had taken their toll!

I was still only one-hundred and fifty pounds, so lightweight crew and one-hundred and fifty-football attracted me. These sports were fun and kept me in good shape. Unlike in high school, I was just mediocre. My first love, basketball, just didn't work out. I was cut on my third workout with the notation: *too short and too slow*. The curriculum of Veterinary school in my third year of college brought the end to my participation in sports. There was just no time!

My career change from General Agriculture to Veterinary Medicine came about as a result of the following circumstances. Traveling to my classes on the upper campus, I often went through the College of Veterinary Medicine. Often there were interesting operations and activities going on which I stopped and observed.

The thought of becoming a Veterinarian suddenly spiked my interest. All students pursuing Vet-med took a pre-vet curriculum and the advisor was J. P. Hertel. I made an appointment to see Professor Hertel. He was very discouraging, explaining that I had taken the basic 101-Chemistry, Botany and Zoology instead of the 105 advanced courses. To make up this deficit, I would have to take these advanced courses, plus Organic Chemistry all in one term. He predicted that I couldn't possibly stay in school with this schedule. This made me all the more determined to try for admission with the minimum of two years of required courses. My advisor in General Agricultural, Stan Warren, encouraged me to go for it, so I went for it. At midterm, I had a ninety-five average and submitted my application to Vet school. They must have thought I was a real brain. These grades, plus my excellent farm background won my acceptance less than two weeks after my interview.

My ninety-five average definitely went down that term, but I did pass all my classes and I was on my way to becoming a Vet.

The second term of my sophomore year I made a terrible mistake that almost cost me my career. A good friend at the SAE fraternity was a freshman and he had his own car. Since freshmen could not have cars on campus, I agreed to register the car in my name. Somehow, the University found out about this and I was called on the carpet. A meeting with Proctor George revealed that I was in serious trouble! He indicated that the matter had to be referred to the faculty committee on student conduct. There was an excellent chance that I would be bounced out of school. My next step was to be interviewed by the chairman of the faculty committee who just happened to be Dr. E. P. Leonard, a prominent professor at the Vet school.

I can still remember walking up the steps of the Small Animal Clinic to his office. With trembling arms and voice, I explained to him that I had just been accepted to the Vet school and begged forgiveness so I could pursue that career. He obviously squashed the charges because I never heard another word. The two people responsible for my career were J. P. Hertel, who said I couldn't do it, and E. P. Leonard, who forgave my indiscretion and let me proceed. So in September of 1953 I entered the freshman class of the NYS Veterinary College at Cornell. It would prove to be four tough years of study. It also opened the gates to a wonderful career working with animals. My life was full speed ahead and there was never a hint of depression or despair in my life. Therefore, it was a shock to all my classmates later in life when they heard that I had attempted suicide. Depression can occur at any age, but there definitely was no indication of it in my younger years.

The first few weeks of Vet school, I was also Rushing Chairman at SAE. This was a busy, busy time. After a rushing luncheon at SAE, I had to hurry back to the Vet school for the lecture on bacteriology, taught by Dorsey Bruner. Invariably, I would arrive late for the lecture and almost immediately fall asleep. When the first exam came up, I had only two pages of notes compared to reams of notes for my classmates. The exam was just ten simple questions—miraculously all of which I was awake for. I received the highest mark in the class, plus considerable ridicule from my classmates. Staying awake when I wasn't physically active was always a problem for me—a holdover from growing up on the farm. I remember the time I borrowed some notes from Mort Howe, a classmate. Halfway through the notes, I fell sound asleep and drooled a fair amount of saliva on the notebook. Later when Mort opened his notes he found about six pages solidly stuck together from the saliva. He never let me borrow his notes again.

We had a secret fraternity in the Vet school called Chi Delta. It was by invitation only and each new class went through an interesting initiation ritual. Everyone would stand in a circle with a pail in the middle. We then would have to *chug a lug* full glasses of beer, one right after another until we had to vomit in the pail. The last one to vomit was the president of the class. We met about once a month at the Richford Hotel a few miles south of Ithaca. This organization not only built lifelong friendships, but also was very instrumental in resolving any problems that arose at the Veterinary school or between the two veterinary fraternities, Alpha Psi and O.T.S. (Omega Tau Sigma). One year I was the Rushing Chairman at Alpha Psi and my good friend Dick Abbott was Rushing Chairman at O.T.S. We mutually agreed to limit the number each house could pledge to twenty-two. Up until that agreement, each class would snowball towards one fraternity, leaving the other fraternity with few pledges and financial problems. This agreement held up for many years and allowed both fraternities to survive. I had many close friends in the O.T.S. fraternity, even though I was an Alpha Psi. One weekend, after a few drinks, I ended up at the O.T.S. National Convention in Canada. Here I was at a banquet of over five-hundred O.T.S. members from all over the country. Luckily no one from Cornell spilled the beans or I would have been tarred and feathered. Today interest in the Vet fraternities has waned. Alpha Psi is now inactive and O.T.S. is active but struggling.

NYS Veterinary College - Cornell 1957 Graduates and Staff

The now James O. Marshall, DVM, circled in the picture

Our class of '57 was one of the last classes with no females. Since then, the fairer sex has taken over the profession and presently two-thirds of the student body is female. Girls consistently present better marks on their applications and more girls apply for admission to vet school than boys. Farm experience is no longer a major requirement for admission and most of the graduates go on to small animal practice, which is more lucrative and much easier than the physically demanding large animal practice.

We had some outstanding professors in the late 1950s. There were Olafson and King in Pathology, Dukes in Physiology, Baker and Whitlock in Parasitology, Hagan and Bruner in Microbiology, Fincher and Fox in Large Animal Medicine, Leonard and Kirk in Small Animal Medicine, McIntee and Roberts in Reproduction, and Danks and Delahanty in Equine Medicine. Dr. Delahanty was a gifted horse Vet who obviously suffered from depression. A few years later he shocked us all by committing suicide.

Of all the professors, Dr. Francis Fox was the most revered by his students. His expertise in bovine medicine and his reputation are world-renowned in this field. The occasion of his birthday was an annual opportunity at the Vet school to play a prank on Dr. Fox. Almost every year his office was dismantled and filled with pigs, sheep, chickens, or other animals. His arrival at the office the next morning was wonderful entertainment. Each year the students would try to out-do the prank of the previous year.

Farm calls with Dr. Fox were an adventure no one wanted to miss. Chewing tobacco or snuff was almost mandatory. He would delight in watching us gag, cough, and sometimes vomit with our first experiences with Copenhagen. We did, however, get the finest instruction in physical diagnosis.

One day, after calls, we all took a boat ride on Cayuga Lake. An intern, Mendel Bartlett, had a nice boat that he kept near Taughannock Farms. Out on the lake, I noticed a pair of water skis in the boat and announced that I could water ski. "Prove it," screamed Dr. Fox. To prove the point, I jumped into the water in my skivvies. Fox was determined to see me fall. When sharp turns failed, they decided to wear me down and took off for Stewart Park eleven miles away. The girls sunning on the docks enjoyed watching a water skier in his skivvies going by. Finally, completely exhausted, I glided into the beach at Stewart Park. I just couldn't let Fox see me fall.

His greatest influence on his students was his special ability to teach the art of physical diagnosis. He would constantly challenge us to evaluate every possible factor and symptom before attempting to make a diagnosis. Today this is almost a lost art as students rush into blood tests, x-rays, sonograms, cat scans, etc. before evaluating the whole picture, and overlook evidence that might contribute to the animal's illness. I'll give you an example of this that occurred later in my professional life.

National Star with his proud owner in 1984

I had a nice racehorse, *National Star*, who developed a small ulcer on his left eye the day before he was scheduled to race. I treated the lesion with ointment and the horse raced well (placing third). The next morning, the eye was worse and appeared to be melting. We rushed him to Cornell where he received round the clock therapy by Dr. Bill Rebhun, an expert in ophthalmology. The horse had picked up a bacterial infection at the track called pseudomonas. This bacterium destroys the eye tissues. After eleven days, the horse was returned to the farm and we continued therapy. A few days later, I held an outing at the farm that included several Veterinary friends, including Dr. Fox and Dr. Rebhun from Cornell. Everyone examined the eye and concluded that the eye would be lost—no hope. Meanwhile, Dr. Fox was walking up and down the stable with his hand working on a large bag of popcorn. His beady eyes were constantly roving the area as they always did when he entered the barn. After a short time, his whiney voice uttered: "Unscrew the light bulb over the horse's stall and darken the stall as much as possible." The bulb was removed and the eye made a dramatic recovery. The horse regained vision; a classic example of the art of physical diagnosis. None of the rest of us had noticed the bulb! The bright light interfered with the healing process.

Dr. Fox still maintains an office at the Veterinary school and I find myself calling him at least once a month with some question. We also try to get together once a year for a golf outing. Dr. Fox never plays but delights in driving the golf cart everywhere, including over the greens and tee areas. Our current foursome is Lew Watson, Byron Parsons, Al Fritz, and me. Our gallery for this exhibition includes Dr. Bob Hillman, an expert in Veterinary Acupuncture and Veterinary Reproductive Medicine and the very beautiful Tracey Brandt, an assistant in Alumni Affairs for the Veterinary College at Cornell. Other golfers that have passed on are Sherm Tharp, Honest Ed Wright, and Dr. Linc Fields.

I could fill this book with stories about Dr. Fox. However, it will be a very sad day when I can no longer call and hear that whiney voice complaining about something.

3

My First Jobs!

All of our classmates had jobs lined up well before graduation. We also had to pass a national written exam and individual practical exam for each state in order to receive a license to practice in the state of our choice. I chose New York, Connecticut, and Massachusetts. I passed New York and Massachusetts, but had to take Connecticut twice before passing.

My first job was working for Dr. Vince Peppe in Canaan, Connecticut. I knew it was a good job because my good friend Dr. Lew Watson worked there the previous year. The job also included membership in the local nine-hole golf course in town. This was a nice signing bonus and several of my classmates were impressed! This job proved to be a great learning experience. The practice served several very wealthy gentlemen farmers who welcomed the very best of professional care for their animals. Cost was not a big factor with them. Also, they welcomed the young vets who came to treat their animals. Sometimes farmers and other old clients are reluctant to use the new graduates. That was not a problem for me in Canaan. There was one farmer client who was a bit of a character. His name was Albert Julian who was about five feet tall, around three-hundred pounds, and boy could he drink. One time, I finished the day with a call to his farm. After the call was finished he invited me up to the house for a drink. I always thought I could hold my own with anyone when it came to alcohol consumption. We started drinking boilermakers and had several. I don't remember leaving his house or driving home to my rooming house. I had to pass several stoplights and a railroad crossing, having no idea whether I stopped or not. This proved that I was no match for Albert and I never tried to keep up with him again.

My boss had a wonderful wife, Shirley, and four kids that were hellions. About twice a month he would get away from the family and the practice. He would take some good books and go to the Jug-End Barn, a nice resort in the Berkshires, for some R&R. I would run the practice and the experience of being on my own was invaluable. In later years, working night and day in my own practice, I would understand the necessity of getting away.

Occasionally Vince would leave me with the practice and the kids to baby-sit while he left with Shirley. This became a real challenge because the kids would be into everything. One day I decided to tell the kids to pretend they were cats and dogs and I locked them all in cages. This worked out great. I could get my work done and I knew exactly where the kids were. When they returned and found all their kids in cages, they weren't too pleased. I never had to baby-sit again.

Playing golf for the first time proved a lot of fun that I would continue to enjoy the rest of my life. One of my first times out, I sliced a ball into the next fairway near some players. One came over and asked, "Why didn't you yell fore?" I answered, "What for?" I did not know the rules of golf.

We also had some interesting cases in the small animal clinic that was attached to his garage. One day a nice gal came in with a canary that had broken its leg. I fashioned a little wooden splint and taped the leg back in the correct position. The splint seemed to work well and the bird walked on the leg right away. The client was very pleased and called later reporting how well the bird was doing. When the bird came back for the splint removal, I was in for a shock. When I removed the tape and splint the whole leg came off with it! The happy client was no longer happy!

Occasionally we would board animals at the clinic. One day a client left her dog to board for two weeks. The dog was very skittish and the first night it climbed over the exercise-run fence. The dog just disappeared and could not be found. I knew where the client lived and would stop by when I was on calls in that area. This was about ten miles from the clinic. About a week later I stopped by the house and there was the dog. Of course he was too shy to come to me. Out of curiosity I tried the front door, and low and behold, it was unlocked. I left the door open and returned to my car. The dog rushed into the house with me right after him. I finally collared him under a bed upstairs. Soon he was back in a cage in the clinic, where I left a note for the kennel man to not let him out without a leash.

This was a happy time. I was making money and I enjoyed golf in the summer and skiing in the winter. The skiing in New England was excellent and I traveled to several different slopes that winter. I also became interested in target shooting at a nearby range. I purchased a .357 Magnum revolver. It is so hard to believe that twenty-eight years later my happiness would change to despair, and I would use this same gun in an attempt to end my life.

In June of 1958, my year was up and I returned home to help out on the farm. My father had suffered a heart attack and my younger brother, Tom, was still in school at Cornell. I did a little vet work around Munnsville, as well as the farm work. One of my first calls was a neighbor's sick dog. I treated the dog using about five dollars' worth of medicine. When the owner asked what my fee was, I replied, "Oh, just pay me what you think it's worth." The neighbor replied, "Well, I certainly think it's worth a dollar." That's the last time I ever let a client determine my fee.

Since my professional life was stagnating, I took a part-time job with a veterinarian about twenty-five miles from the farm. When my brother returned to help run the farm, I started looking for a location to open my own practice. Also, at this same time, a serious relationship developed in my life for the first time. I fell madly in love with a beautiful girl named Gretchen. We planned to marry in the fall. About a month before the wedding, we attended her company's annual picnic. At the party, she became very jealous when I danced with some of her friends, and she left with my car and without me. This really ticked me off since I had to hire a taxi to get home. Suddenly, I had second thoughts and called off the wedding.

Now my life was devastated and my first experience with depression set in. The practice I was working for held no future, my love life had been shattered, and I was turned down on my plans to build a hospital on a nice location in nearby Manlius. All my dreams were shattered so I decided to take a job with Dr. Willard Daniels in Guilford, Connecticut.

With tears streaming down my face, I loaded all my earthly possessions in my car and took off for my next job. This actually turned out to be a terrific move for me. Will Daniels was a terrific boss, the practice was great, and I soon had many enjoyable new friends. The depression lifted and happiness returned.

Guilford was a delightful town to live in. I found an apartment in town for thirty-five dollars a month. It was up a long stairway and had only one window. However, this was fine since I only needed a place to sleep. My salary was eleven thousand dollars a year, which in those days was a fortune. My social life was plenty active. When I wasn't working I was out on the town. Not too much of my salary went into my savings.

The practice consisted of a very busy small animal hospital, plus a good number of farm accounts. I really enjoyed the large animal calls, and was readily accepted as a country vet. My favorite calls involved reproduction in the bovine (cows). There were several excellent Holstein herds in the area. The Auger family owned several farms and they all had excellent herds. A cow is the most profitable to its owner if they have a calf every twelve months. Since the pregnancy takes nine months, the cow should be bred back about three months after she freshens (has a baby). A good veterinarian can be very helpful with frequent examinations (with the long glove). Most farmers realize that cow reproduction is by far their biggest need for a vet.

Other common problems for the dairy farmer that require a vet are milk fever (hypocalcaemia), calving problems (dystocia), ketosis (acetonemia), cast withers (prolapse of the uterus), and infected feet.

Milk fever occurs at calving time. The sudden onset of milk production drains the body of calcium causing muscle weakness and paralysis. Often the cow is flat out and appears close to death. The intravenous administration of a calcium solution results in a dramatic cure with the cow standing up after treatment. In some herds, this is a common problem and the farmers have learned to treat these cases themselves.

Calving problems can be very physically challenging. Normally, a foal or calf is delivered without assistance. The head and front feet come first in a normal delivery. In some cases, the head or feet fold back into the uterus making delivery impossible. Most farmers attempt to deliver the newborn themselves. When they are unsuccessful, they call the vet. When you get one of these calls, you know you're in for a workout because they take care of the easy ones. The delivery involves a baby that weighs seventy to one-hundred pounds, so physical strength is a requirement! Usually we have to inject an anesthetic (epidural) into the spinal canal to relax the muscles. This stops the powerful contractions and allows us to reposition the newborn for delivery. The worst cases are the ones where the baby has died and remained in the uterus for a few days. In this situation, the baby is badly swollen and infected. This requires an embryotomy (cutting off legs or a head) or a cesarean. Saving the mother in these situations is a real challenge.

Another physically challenging condition is Cast Withers. This occurs following delivery when the cow or mare keeps straining violently, causing the uterus to prolapse out of the body. Often the animal is down with the prolapsed uterus hanging over the gutter, covered with filth. If the mother can stand up, correction is much easier. First an epidural anesthetic has to be administered to stop the straining. Then the uterus needs to be washed as clean as possible. Next, the uterus has to be supported with a board (assistant on each side), while the veterinarian pushes the organ back into the normal position. The vulva is then sutured to prevent a reoccurrence when the anesthetic wears off. Believe me, after one of these cases, you need to go home for a hot shower and clean clothes.

One of my favorite stops was the Neubig Farm. The Neubigs were a wonderful German family that worked together running their large dairy farm. Later, when I decided to return to New York to open my own practice, the Neubigs let me use their workshop, where I constructed kennels for my future hospital. I spent many hours working there and they wouldn't accept a dime in return. It's been forty years and some of these kennels that I made at the Neubigs are still in use at the Fayetteville Veterinary Hospital.

My boss in Guilford, Dr. Willard Daniels, was a great vet and a wonderful guy. He was one of the happiest men I have ever met, and he had a likeable circle of friends, all of whom I got to know. I don't know how he could do it, but he could party until 4:00 a.m. and be at work raring to go at 7:00 a.m. I tried to stay with him one night and dragged into work at noon. The two years I worked in Guilford bring back fond memories. If I had stayed one more year, I would probably still be there. A year later Willard decided to take a job at the University of Connecticut. He sold the practice to Dr. Dave Anderson, who replaced me in the practice.

One of the great families of Guilford that I loved was the Page family. Harry Page, Sr. was my first landlord who rented me an apartment for thirty-five dollars a month. When I first moved in, several of the Pages gave me a hand in carrying everything up that long, narrow stairway. After the apartment was settled, I broke out a gallon of hard cider that I had brought down from "York State." Soon everyone was slurring their words and the Pages felt well compensated for their efforts. Getting back down the stairs was a bit of an effort, but everyone made it. They really liked that cider from "York State."

Harry Page, Jr. and his wife, Hazel, were terrific people. The Page family ran *Page Hardware* on the green in Guilford, which was successful and the family was well regarded. I'm pretty sure *Page Hardware* is still in the family and operating today.

Harry owned a nice summerhouse on Circle Beach in Madison right on Long Island Sound. It was a beautiful spot and rented for a thousand dollars a month, which in those days was a tidy sum. When he heard some friends and relatives were visiting me over Memorial Day weekend (1960), he offered the beach house to me for free. My sister Zoe and her husband Ed were coming down from Haverhill, Massachusetts, and a friend of theirs, Dick Burke, was coming up from Morristown, New Jersey. Dick was also bringing his sister Ruthie. Although I was not ready for another serious relationship, I soon fell madly in love with Ruthie, and less than a year later we were married. There was no living together back in those days. Ruthie came up every weekend from New Jersey and stayed with the

Daniels. She went on several calls with me and attended several deliveries. After witnessing some tough deliveries using the obstetrical chains, it's a wonder that she wanted to have children. Our romance blossomed and December 3, 1960, we announced our engagement with a nice party at the Morristown School in Morristown, New Jersey. The following April fifteenth we were married in Florham Park, New Jersey. The reception was at the Morris County Golf Club and all had a good time. All my pals from Guilford were there and the bar was very busy. Harry Page, Sr. kept falling down on the dance floor. Every time he fell, he complained that people were leaving their olive pits on the floor, and that's what tripped him up.

Harry Page was a fun-loving guy that everyone loved. Several years later, I received the sad news that he became despondent and ended his life with a gunshot to the head. This tragic loss, plus Dr. Delahanty, together with my own experience with depression, has driven me to develop *Jim Marshall Farms*, a place where animals can help people with depression (before it's too late.)!

After the wedding, we were off to Bermuda for our honeymoon. We had a nice honeymoon cottage at Ariel Sands. The first disagreement of our married life occurred over the motorbikes that you just have to ride if you go to Bermuda. Ruthie got scared riding a bike and couldn't keep up. She stopped on the road where a native was working. The native proceeded to tell her how many people had been killed on motorbikes. We solve then dilemma by returning the two bikes and exchanging for a bike that was built for two. She agreed to ride on the back, so everything was rosy again. The shops in Bermuda are noted for their fine china and crystal. I was smoking and chewing cigars at the time. When I pulled the cigar that I was chewing out of my mouth, a large piece soaked in saliva plopped onto a piece of Royal Dalton. The clerk and my wife were horrified. At that point, the only way to be forgiven was to buy the china, which I did.

We returned to our special honeymoon cottage on the Post Road in Madison, Connecticut, which we rented from the Shaeffers. One of our wedding presents was a Chesapeake Bay puppy we called *Lancer*. He turned out to be a terrific dog we would enjoy for the next fourteen years. One of my favorite pastimes was duck hunting. I had a little skiff and motor and would go out early mornings to the Hammonasset Park that was only a couple miles from our house. *Lancer* loved the water and as soon as I had all the decoys in place, he would swim out and bring them all back to the shore. One time I shot a duck, which he retrieved beautifully. Instead of bringing the bird to me, he proceeded to chew it to bits. A great hunting dog he was not! *Lancer* was our first son and accompanied us everywhere. Once we had to go away to a wedding and had to leave him in a cage in the hospital. When we returned two days later, he sat in the back seat looking out the back window. He didn't forgive us for two days. In later years with my own practice, he was always wandering around the waiting room and everyone adored him. One day a client came in and asked, "Where's *Lancer* today, Dr. Mitchell?" They knew *Lancer* better than me.

Working in Guilford and the surrounding towns were happy times. Now that I was married, my carefree single days behind me, I started thinking about my own practice. Since all my roots were in Central New York, I decided to check out the eastern suburbs of Syracuse. I wanted to have a mixed practice consisting of both farm animals and a hospital for companion pets.

Finding a location to build an animal hospital was easier said than done. I wrote to all the large real estate offices in Syracuse and came up with nothing attractive. Downtown was just not acceptable to a farm boy like me, and in the suburbs no one wanted an animal hospital next door. We would drive up from Connecticut with high hopes and return Sunday night dejected. Finally, in desperation, I started knocking on doors when I spotted an attractive location. My big break came when I met George Bender at his home. He owned about ninety acres and had just sold a parcel to Dave Watts on Route 5 (two miles east of Fayetteville) for a boarding kennel. Zoning was no problem since my only neighbors were a kennel on one side and a quarry on the other. The only problem was the price of five thousand dollars, which, at that time, was an astronomical sum of money! My father and Uncle Fred agreed to help out financially, so I closed the deal. Returning to Connecticut, we were aglow with the anticipation of starting our own practice.

About a month later, after resigning my wonderful job in Guilford, I received the news that Dr. Stack, a prominent veterinarian in Syracuse, was opening in Fayetteville only two miles from my location. I was distraught! The prospect of two hospitals succeeding in this small town was unlikely. Mine would surely fail, since Dr. Stack was already established. My wonderful job was filled with my replacement, our honeymoon cottage was already rented, Ruth was pregnant with our first child, and all my money was invested in the one acre of land in Fayetteville. Woe was me! I remember so well the words of my father when I called him with this development. He said, "Well, Jim, if you're afraid of competition, you'll be running the rest of your life!" With this advice, I forgot about being a wimp and decided to go for it in Fayetteville. With all our earthly treasures in Charlie Scranton's farm truck, we left all our dear friends in Connecticut and journeyed to Munnsville where we lived with my parents while our home/hospital was being built. It was Memorial Day weekend, 1962.

4

Off On My Own

My farm rearing came in handy with the construction process. You learn to be an architect, carpenter, plumber, mason, and general contractor. I knew just what I wanted. One wing facing Route 5 would be the hospital, and the other wing would be our living quarters with the garage in between. In those days, just about every veterinarian lived right next to the clinic, if not in the same building. It was like the old New England homesteads where the house and stables were connected. In hindsight, it was a mistake to be that close to your work. Clients would assume you were there and would stop in whenever they felt like it.

Ruth was heavily pregnant and stayed with my mother in Munnsville. Father, Uncle Fred, and I would leave for Fayetteville at daybreak and usually wouldn't return until dark. It was pretty much a do-it-yourself project. We had two carpenters, Rex and Stew Touse, an electrician, Fred Bennett, and we did pretty much everything else.

In 1962 on the night of July seventeenth, Ruth woke me up to call the doctor. She recalls that I told the doctor, "My wife is leaking fluid." It sounded to her like I was calling a mechanic about a car problem. The next morning at 5:00 a.m. we became parents. James Otis Marshall, Jr. had arrived in good health. He would be called Otey from that moment on and would graduate from Princeton twenty-two years later.

Construction proceeded slowly but surely. I had a chance to get a fabulous discount on a heating system, but only if I did it myself. Since there were no calls to go on yet, I became a plumber and put the entire system in (and it worked). There were no utilities, so we had to drill a well and put in a septic tank. Unfortunately, the well proved to be sulphur water and we never got used to the smell of rotten eggs. By this time, word was getting out that a farm vet was available and I started getting some income, which was very much needed.

Finally, on November 3, 1962, our family of three moved into our new home/ hospital facility. With a beautiful five-inch snowfall covering the landscape, we were for the first time completely on our own. Our first dinner menu was pork chops, and boy were they good! As our family and practice grew, we would add on to the building four different times. We would live here, raising four children, for the next eighteen years. I was full of ambition, purpose, dedication to family, active in the profession, church and community, and determined to succeed. There was never a hint of the depression that would totally consume my zest for life twenty-two years later.

One of my very first clients wanted to board their German Sheperd for a few days. Since my outside runs were still under construction, I was using a portable run that the dog immediately escaped from. We were devastated. The dog ran up the road, which was busy with traffic, and would return to the hospital about every hour looking for its owner. Every hour we could see the dog in the road, as the lights of the cars would go by. Finally, at three in the morning, the dog came in the rear door of the hospital I left open (with food) and was captured. Completely exhausted, we fell into bed. Was this what your own practice was going to be like? We were experiencing stress!

Dr. Stack and I opened our hospitals at about the same time. Since he was well established in Syracuse, most all of my first clients thought my new hospital was Dr. Stack's. When the doorbell would ring, I rushed out with great anticipation, only to direct the client to Dr. Stack's office.

Although the practice started out very slowly, I did stay busy finishing the hospital construction. The early income was meager, but I did save a lot on expenses by doing it myself. Professional fees were extremely low. An office call was three dollars compared to the twenty-five to thirty-five dollars today.

Gradually we settled into life in Fayetteville. Most of our close friends were made after attending the Fayetteville Methodist Church. We met the Hummel, Hiller, Noyes, and Osborne families, who are still close friends forty years later. I joined the Fayetteville Jaycees and we met several more young couples. Everyone was struggling to survive starting his or her families and careers. We all seemed to have fun without spending a lot of money, which all of us were short of. It was a few years before I could afford to put a concrete floor in the garage. Nevertheless, we held parties there from time to time. On one wall, I built a huge reel that held a large rug we would hit golf balls into. When not in use, I rolled it up to the ceiling like a window shade. We had a cheap pool table that also was pulled up to the ceiling out of the way when it was not in use. On another wall, I had a large screen on which was painted a beautiful curvaceous pin-up girl with large breasts. One of our games was to unroll this screen and using two balloons with tacks, while blindfolded, play "*Pin the Boobies on Buella.*" Could you imagine hosting a party today in a garage with a dirt floor? We proved that young people could have a good time without spending a fortune.

About once a month, several of us would get together in the evening for food, beer, and poker. One time we were meeting at our house and Ted Hiller's luck was running bad. After losing several hands in a row, he announced that twenty dollars was more money than he could afford to lose. We'd all had a few beers and tried to talk him into a few more hands, but he had had enough and walked out the door. A few minutes later the doorbell rang. It seems Ted, in his anguish, had backed his little Renault into a huge ditch and was stuck. One front wheel was clearly eighteen inches off the ground. At this point, everyone was feeling no pain and we announced to Ted that it would be another twenty dollars to push him back on the road. We really didn't charge him.

Several years later, while attending a party at Ted's house in Fayetteville, we all congregated in their living room after dinner. Ted's wife, Ruth, is an immaculate housekeeper and their home is absolutely beautiful. For some reason, one of the guests, Henry Drake, decided that I just had to examine his dog that evening and left the party to get his dog and return to the Hillers. When he brought the dog into the house without a leash, it was so excited to see all the people that it ran around the living room several times urinating every step of the way. Everyone had some dog urine on their shoes and socks. There also were brown streaks decorating Ruth's beautiful furniture and rug. It's been about forty years since that party, but we still laugh about it whenever we get together.

Living next to the hospital had its advantages when it came to emergencies. I had a buzzer installed just outside our bedroom. By flipping a switch, the front doorbell to the hospital would activate this buzzer. I really built my small animal practice by taking care of people's emergencies. They would truly appreciate this service and would return with all their entire routine vet needs later. Clients appreciated the after-hours service and as the word spread, my practice grew. When someone called with an emergency (usually hit by a car), I stayed in bed until the buzzer went off. Often the dog or cat would die before reaching the hospital and the client wouldn't show up (to save money). With this arrangement, I kept on sleeping in these cases.

One winter evening, about midnight, the buzzer went off. It was a gorgeous client in a maxi coat and her sick dog. Following an examination, I concluded that the dog had to be admitted. Leaving the client with her dog in the exam room, I left to prepare the kennel in intensive care for admission. When I returned, in addition to the client in the maxi coat and the dog, there was a lady's nightgown on the exam table with the dog. She explained that she wanted an article of her clothing to be left with the dog. It suddenly dawned on me that she had removed her nightgown while I had prepared the kennel and had nothing on under the coat. I felt like asking, "Can I take your coat, Ma'am?"

Thirty years later, we met again at a cocktail party on Squirrel Island off the coast of Maine. She remembered the office visit and we had a good laugh.

Holidays were no exception for emergencies. One Christmas Eve the buzzer went off while we were preparing for Santa's visit. It was Jim D'Amico, a good friend with his young son and Golden Retriever who had been hit by a car. A drunken Santa Claus, speeding through a residential area, drove the car. My daughter Cynthia came over to the office to give me a hand. The dog was in shock with extensive internal injuries.

We had a happy result. The dog made a complete recovery, but Jim's young son's respect for Santa Claus had been shattered!

With the house adjacent to the hospital, the kids and our own pets were constant visitors. Our Chesapeake Bay retriever, *Lancer*, roamed the hospital all the time. He really thought he was a big shot having his freedom when all the clients' dogs were on leashes. Everyone knew his name and he never was a problem.

Lancer was very jealous of our neighbor's Collie, *Tay*. Whenever *Tay* would wander over to our property, *Lancer* would beat him up. One time, while in the middle of office hours, the kids ran in screaming that *Lancer* had killed *Tay*. When I arrived at the scene on our back lawn, there was a pool of blood but no dog. I followed the trail of blood up the hill and found *Tay* collapsed just outside our neighbor's house. Without alerting the neighbor (who I could see inside their house), I carried *Tay* back to the hospital and into intensive care. After treatment with blood transfusions and shock treatment, *Tay* stabilized. I then called the neighbors and explained what had happened. Finally, after another week of free treatment, *Tay* went home. This scenario would happen again a few months later. After the second hospitalization, *Tay* finally decided against future visits to *Lancer's* domain.

Occasionally our cat, *Peppermint*, would also visit the hospital. One day a client came in with a beautiful golden canary with striking plumage. They asked if I had a quiet place in the hospital to board the caged bird away from the dogs. I replied that the bird could stay in my office on the desk. The second day *Peppermint* somehow found her way into the office and spent the night reaching into the cage and cuffing the bird with her claws. The next morning, the beautiful bird was completely bald except for one feather sticking out its rear end. I explained to the owners that the feathers would probably grow back in time. As you would guess, we never saw the bird or the client ever again.

One January, a client brought his English Setter into the hospital to board for two days and be wormed. The only problem was that he never returned to pick up the dog. After endless phone calls and registered letters, the dog was legally abandoned and we were free to dispose of it however we wished. By this time, everyone was in love with this beautiful animal and we kept it as a hospital mascot. The following September, the first day of hunting season, the client returned and announced, "Well, Jim, I'm here to pick up my dog." I knew he was a deadbeat, but he had a check signed by his wife who had some money. Using poor judgment, I discharged the dog before seeing if the check was any good. Sure enough, the check bounced! The teller at the bank knew the story and felt sorry for us. We called her every morning for two weeks and there were no funds to cover the check. About a week later, she called asking us to get the check there ASAP. Ruth rushed to the bank and we finally had the money!

In 1963, Cynthia Lee arrived December eleventh, complete with red hair and a temperament to match. We have a priceless piece of film of her parading around our deck in diapers with one of my cigars dangling from her mouth. She received a good bit of notoriety by throwing a toy truck and hitting Uncle Fred in the head. With blood running down his forehead, Uncle Fred announced that he'd had enough of Cynthia Lee and was planning to go home. Fortunately, he reconsidered and stayed with us. His help was invaluable in the early days building the hospital and practice. My clients loved *Lancer* and Uncle Fred! He would sit in the waiting room for hours visiting with the clients about their pets and how things were in the old days.

About this time, more animals arrived on our estate. I purchased two pregnant ewes (sheep) from Dr. Danks at Cornell. A pasture was created on the hill behind the hospital and we would have lambs in the spring. Father brought over an old brooder house from the farm for use as a lamb house and later stable for our ponies. Cynthia became very attached to the sheep and would feed them daily out of her bedroom window. They loved saltine crackers and our grocery bill went up. When it came time for slaughter, she was devastated. Even to this day, she will not eat lamb.

There was no time for days off or vacations. It would be seven years before we were able to take a week off to go to our beloved Squirrel Island off the coast of Boothbay Harbor, Maine. After a slow start, the practice started to grow and I became very busy. Twelve-to-fourteen-hour days were routine. The clients liked evening office hours. Since I was willing to work till 8:00 p.m. five days a week, the word spread and the clients were attracted to my practice.

Horse and farm calls were hard to work in as the hospital practice grew. One day in the middle of a busy afternoon of office hours, I received a call from a client in Syracuse whose pet Beagle, *George*, had cut his tail. An artery was severed at the tip of his tail and was spraying blood all over the white carpets in their beautiful home. *George*, who had a nasty disposition, would growl when anyone would attempt to bandage his tail. Finally, the owner, a prominent professional, had been called home, canceling his one-hundred dollar-per-hour appointments to attend to *George*. He also was scared to death to approach *George*. The doctor called the office and pleaded with me to come to the house. After juggling the appointments, I drove to the house where I found the doctor, his family, and neighbors all helplessly watching *George* sitting on the white carpet with blood spraying all over. When I approached *George*, he growled and showed his teeth to me. After administering a stiff slap across *George's* nose, he changed his attitude and I was able to apply a bandage and take *George* back to the hospital for sutures.

The doctor and his wife did not believe in using physical discipline for their children or pets. I think I proved the point that occasional physical discipline for unacceptable behavior can be very effective for animals as well as children. Their children were also uncontrollable and trashed our waiting room on every visit. I've often wondered how the kids turned out.

It soon became obvious that the hospital was too small. After spending another fortune for additional land to the west, we added three more kennel rooms, an office, plus an apartment for help in the lower level. Our neighbor's son, Ed Gridley, who is a terrific mechanic, welded together all the kennels. Our clients preferred to board their pets at our hospital and over Thanksgiving and other holiday vacations; we would have eighty pets in residence. That's a lot of barking in the morning at feeding time.

One year our assessment for taxes went up and I decided to challenge the increase. After making a recording of all the barking, I made an appointment with the grievance board of six to eight prominent citizens. I explained that living that close to a hospital was not Park Place and asked them to listen to the sounds we hear every morning outside our dining room window. The tape recorder then blared the loud sound of the barking dogs. Soon they begged me to turn off the tape recording and they lowered the assessment. I had made my point.

By 1964, it was obvious that we needed more living space. We added three more bedrooms and a bath. Our third child was on the way and I still felt that it was necessary to live close to the practice. One Sunday afternoon, I was painting one of the new bedrooms and became very tired. After flopping down on the bed for a brief nap, I opened my eyes to what I first thought was a bad dream. Our three-year-old son, Otey, in his *Doctor Dentons*, had decided to help his poor tired dad out with the painting. He had dipped the roller into the paint (light beige) and proceeded to paint the walls, the furniture, and the brand new blue rug. He couldn't understand why I was upset. Fortunately it was latex paint.

On November 10, 1965, Peter John arrived. November 8th was the black-out that affected the whole Northeast. By the time of Peter's arrival, fortunately, the lights were back on. This was also the first winter I would experience depression. S.A.D., which stands for Seasonal Affective Disorder, affects millions during the winter months when sunlight (especially in Syracuse) is almost non-existent. The winter blues make the Christmas holidays a very unhappy time for S.A.D. patients.

I remember the Christmas of 1965 returning from a family get-together in Munnsville. While driving home, I started to sob uncontrollably. It was a scary experience for Ruth, who had three small children to care for and a husband who had apparently lost control. I recovered in a few hours, but this was the first sign of an illness that would devastate my later life. Over the next twelve years, the winter blues would leave me somber, but I was able to function okay.

There never is a routine day in a general practice of veterinary medicine, especially when farm calls are involved. The first calls came in between 4:30 and 5:30 a.m. when the dairy farmers first came into their barns. These are always emergency situations that require immediate attention. Calving difficulties are the most common along with cast withers and milk fever. Farmers work long, hard hours and they expect the vet to do the same. You just don't tell them to give their cow an aspirin and call you later in the day. In the early days of my practice, large animal calls comprised more than fifty percent of the practice. Fayetteville was a rapidly growing suburb of Syracuse. Most of my farm clients sold out to housing developments. The small animal practice grew rapidly while the farm practice dwindled.

After a 7:30 a.m. breakfast, I would be in the hospital at eight when we opened. The animal health technician (AHT) would prepare a work sheet for all the day's work. AHTs were just coming into existence at that time. It is an excellent career for a young person. They are invaluable to a busy practice. Over the years, I would have several excellent AHTs who were almost like having another vet on staff. By nine, all of the large animal calls would be in. When the hospital treatments and surgeries were finished, I would take off on the calls hoping to be back for office hours at one in the afternoon. Later, when I had the luxury of an associate vet, one of us would be at the hospital at all times.

On January 17, 1969, Jennifer Ruth, who would be our last child, was born. A few years later, the sheep were replaced with a pony, *Princess*, and a small Arab mare, *Shadow*. The lamb house became a two-stall stable. The kids loved the horses. Jennifer would spend every possible moment with *Princess* and Cynthia would ride *Shadow*.

On every Memorial Day, Fayetteville hosts a parade, which passes through the village. Jennifer wanted to ride *Princess* in the parade. The pony would go anywhere, so I loaded her into my practice van and we were off to the parade. People would stop and stare, watching a van go by with a horse's head sticking out the window. Jen made it up the parade route with *Princess* and was in seventh heaven.

In 1971, we added a swimming pool and small pool house on the back corner of our property. The kids were ecstatic with their own pool. A few years later, we added three bedrooms to the pool house and this became our summer house which was just three-hundred feet south of our winter house. We were a happy family with our dog *Lancer* and cat *Reckless*, and two horses, *Princess* and *Shadow*. Depression and despair were certainly not a worry at this point in my life.

One morning, a client arrived with the news that a yellow cat (possibly *Reckless*) was smashed on the road in front of the hospital. The cat appeared to be *Reckless*, but had been run over several times making identification difficult. Since *Reckless* was declawed in front, I knew that if the dead cat had no front claws, it would be *Reckless*. Sure enough, upon careful examination, the dead cat had been declawed and had to be *Reckless*. I reported the death to the family and everyone cried and cried. About an hour later, the real *Reckless* walked in the back door. The kids shrieked with joy and *Reckless* was deluged with love and affection. It had obviously been a *Reckless* look-alike that had met death in the road.

Clint and Mary Getty were wonderful clients whose life revolved around their cat *Puddy*. On one occasion, they left *Puddy* with us to board for a few days. Due to some construction, a cat run was left open and *Puddy* escaped. The cat was last seen running into the woods behind the hospital. When they returned, I had to break the tragic news to them. They asked to be shown where *Puddy* was last seen and walked up to the edge of the woods. It had been over a week, and I was sure the cat was long gone. They started calling "Here *Puddy*, Here *Puddy*" which I thought was a waste of time. After about the fourth "Here *Puddy*," the cat ran out of the woods and jumped into their arms. Of all the happy people, I was the happiest. They are terrific people, and believe it or not, still wanted to pay me for the boarding.

Good employees are a major part of a successful small animal hospital operation. The way they answer the phone and greet the clients makes a lasting good or bad impression. The clients love to be recognized and be on a first-name basis with the receptionists, technicians, and even the kennel people. On one occasion, the impression was not so good. A prominent and wealthy potential client stopped in one morning and asked if she could meet Dr. Marshall. The receptionist invited her to wait in exam room one. I introduced myself and we seemed to be hitting it off. She had several pets and was considering changing veterinarians. After I had reviewed our services and policies, I told her about the wonderful caring staff we had at the hospital. At this point, we started to hear a voice through the air conditioning duct overhead. The duct connected directly to the grooming room where the groomer was trying to give a dog a haircut. "You dirty little bastard. If you don't hold still, I'll kick your ass." I raised my voice, but the groomer's tirade was still very audible. More profanity continued, "Hold still or I'll knock your f—ing head off." My favorable impression had gone down the drain. The potential client left—never to return. I immediately went down to the grooming room and fired the groomer.

Another employee was late for work on a regular basis. She always had an excuse. The alarm didn't go off, the car wouldn't start, the garage door was stuck shut, I lost my keys, all sorts of medical reasons—every day a different excuse. One day I exclaimed, "What's the excuse today?" She replied, "Doc, it was the birds! There were so many birds in the road, I couldn't get through." She apparently got the idea from Alfred Hitchcock's movie, *The Birds*. That is my all-time favorite excuse. Whenever I'm late getting home, I just tell my wife, "It was the birds!"

Often I took the kids with me on farm calls. The main attraction was not the farm call, but the stop for ice cream on the way home. Cynthia was absolutely fearless of the many barn cats each farm would have. Most of them were wild and never handled by humans. They were kept to keep the rat population down. As soon as we entered the barn, she would pick up the nearest cat and pet it. The farmers would be shocked, reporting, "No one could ever touch that cat." I can't remember her ever getting a scratch.

Unfortunately, none of my children was interested in pursuing a career in veterinary medicine. I think they were turned off with all the hours I worked in the practice. Few vets start their own practice from scratch any more and tend to work in group practices with regular hours and plenty of time off. I'm still hoping one of my grandchildren or great-grandchildren will choose this great profession and become a vet.

The Fayetteville-Manlius Jaycees were very active at that time. We not only met several wonderful couples that became lifelong friends, but also rendered service to the community. The Jaycees organized the Memorial Day parade as well as several other community projects. It was my suggestion that we place the horse and carriages and all the riding horses at the end of the parade. This way, the band, boy scouts, girl scouts, and little leaguers didn't have to trudge through the road apples.

Through the Jaycees, we met the Tracys, who operated the local lumberyard, and the Elliotts. They have been close friends for forty years. Chuck Elliott was our local physician and truly a great asset to the community. We love to share stories of our early practice days when we were together. I love the one he tells about *Gus the Greek* who ran a local restaurant at that time. It seems that Gus cut his finger one day and came to Chuck's office to have the cut sutured and bandaged. About a week later, Chuck was enjoying a bowl of chili at Gus' place. The chili was delicious, but halfway through the bowl, Chuck was reunited with the bandage he had placed on Gus' finger a week earlier. Suddenly the chili didn't taste so good.

Chuck likes to tell the story of his first job at Louie Wilson's animal hospital in Syracuse. On the first day of work, Chuck was instructed to put the dogs in outside runs and clean the cages. After the dogs were back in, Chuck thought the cats needed some fresh air, so he put them out in the dog runs. The runs were not covered and the cats were soon over the fence and out on their own—never to be seen again. As soon as Dr. Wilson received this news, Chuck was immediately fired. This experience helped direct his career from animals to people.

I worked my way up in the Jaycees and became president in 1965. On one occasion, I had to present Tom Osborne with an award. When he reached the front of the room and stood waiting for his award, I said, "Tom, turn your head and cough!" This broke up the meeting, and even to this day, almost forty years later, when I see Tom at a party, his favorite words are, "Turn your head and cough!" Tom was an engineer who has a brilliant mind. Shortly after this incident, Tom had a calling to medicine and went off to med school. Tom's wife, Sharon, went to work as a nurse and supported the family through those tough years of medical school. Often you hear these stories of the working wife putting her husband through Med school, only to have the doctor later run off with a pretty young nurse. Not so with Tom and Sharon. They are happily married with five children and thirteen grandchildren. Tom is a prominent physician in nearby Cazenovia. Now when patients arrive at his office, he says, "Turn your head and cough!"

At age thirty-five, you're out of the Jaycees, so along with Chuck Elliott, I became a charter member of the Fayetteville-Manlius Rotary Club. We met every Wednesday for lunch. I used to bring little treasures from the practice for surprises to certain members for their lunch. One of the most popular servings (after a morning call to castrate a horse) was testicle under glass. The normal horse testicle is the size of a grapefruit. Another gem was a striking necklace created with ten puppy dog tails. I presented the necklace to the president to be worn proudly as our exalted leader.

In 1971, I was elected president of the Rotary, which was a distinct honor. One of the toughest jobs in Rotary is to find good program speakers for each weekly meeting. Chuck Elliott was my program chairman and arranged fifty-two programs during my year as president.

Our pool house was the site of several New Year's Eve parties. We had ice skating on the pool, as well as sledding down a nearby hill on flying saucers. Two things you can plan on in Syracuse for New Year's Eve are cold weather and lots of snow. After the outdoor activities, we all returned to the pool house for dinner and celebrating the New Year. One year I made some glug which was tasty but extremely potent. It took its toll! One of our friends was found wandering around the parking lot looking for his mother. Another friend had trouble putting one foot in front of the other. When it came time to leave, he needed assistance to get to the car. The only problem was that the assistants were almost as bad as he was. The same night Ruth had made some brownies that turned out rock hard and were impossible to chew. Soon the brownies were being hurled back and forth among the participants. It was hard to find a designated driver!

About this time I became interested in motorcycles. I bought a used cycle, took my driving test, and failed. It seems I lacked experience and wiped out on a curb while taking the test. My second attempt went better and I passed with flying colors. Certain farm calls requiring only my medical bag were made on the cycle. It is a lot of fun to drive a cycle, but very dangerous. One night I was out on the road and a drunk driver nearly pulled in front of me coming out of a tavern. The cycle was going about 60 miles an hour. The car stopped just inches short of hitting me. This was too close a brush with death. I gave up driving on the road as soon as I got home.

In 1965, I became a charter member of the *Cavalry Golf Club* in Manlius. Some troopers from the Cavalry Corp of World War I bought some beautiful farm land in Manlius about 1904. They had stables there and would ride over bridle paths for recreation. I treated horses there and also attended horse shows held on the property. They converted the farmhouse into an eating club, which became very popular. By 1965, there were nine-hundred members with a very long waiting list. The younger generation of troopers enjoyed golf more than riding horses and voted to convert the property into a golf course. For a very short time, there was a problem enlisting members for the golf club. A nearby proposed golf course, *The Ledges*, had failed and several people had lost their money. Bill Bushong, one of the original organizers, was a good client of mine and convinced me to come up with two-hundred dollars to become a charter member. The course has matured into one of the finest courses in New York State. Although I am far from being a good golfer, membership has been a luxury we have enjoyed now for over thirty-five years.

If you live in the Northeast you have to learn to ski. The winters are long and rugged with ten to fifteen feet of snowfall every winter. I had started skiing during my last two years at Cornell. A bunch of us went up to Stowe, Vermont, and learned to ski the hard way—lots of bumps and bruises. In those days, skiing was very affordable. We stayed in a house in town where the owner had built several double bunk beds in his basement where we stayed overnight for a dollar a night, including breakfast. One person of our group snuck out in the morning without paying (one of the most dishonest acts I ever witnessed). Later, after settling in Fayetteville, skiing helped us get through the winters. We joined *Cazenovia Ski Club*, which was nearby and very affordable. It was a family-oriented facility and many of our friends were members. All of our kids learned to ski there with no major injuries except for our Peter. I had an old pair of skis with cable bindings that didn't release causing Peter to fracture his tibia. After that experience, I insisted on the best equipment for everyone—expensive but safe. Now that I'm approaching seventy, I still try to ski at least once a year. Our niece and nephew have a beautiful condominium at Okemo Mountain in Vermont. This is a wonderful spot to spend a winter weekend. The force of gravity gets me down the hill very well, but getting back up after a fall is a major problem. Although it is now very expensive, with equipment and lift tickets, skiing is one of the finest family sports. (I now ski with my grandchildren.)

The winter of 1966 produced one of the worst snowstorms in my memory. The snowdrifts were eight to ten feet deep. The snow on the east side of our house completely covered the first floor windows and front door, and went all the way up to the windows of the second floor. We had to tunnel our way out of the house. It took us a couple of days to get dug out. The farmers came by and picked me up to get to their farms for vet work since I couldn't get my practice vehicle out of the garage. We were fortunate to have the *Kinsella Quarry* next door. They have been great neighbors for forty years. In the '66 storm, they came over with a huge pay loader to clear the snow out. We were back in business.

5

The 1970s

Adding an associate veterinarian to the practice was a welcome milestone in our lives. Our first associate was Dr. Joe Haddad, a Cornell graduate. I now had the luxury of some occasional time off and an actual vacation. In August, I cleaned out all the medications from my white Ford practice van, replaced them with a foam rubber pad for the kids to sleep on and we were off to Squirrel Island.

Squirrel Island is a very special and delightful spot three miles out in the Atlantic, off Boothbay Harbor, Maine. It is an eight and a half hour drive from Syracuse, but well worth the effort once you get there. The Island was settled in the 1800s and early 1900s. About one-hundred summer cottages have been built along with a chapel, a town hall, teashop, post office, library, and five excellent clay tennis courts. A hotel attracted guests for many years but burned to the ground in 1962. No cars or bicycles are allowed. People move about on sidewalks that encircle the Island. A couple of trucks carry luggage and supplies to the cottages from the Nellie Dock where a ferry arrives from the mainland. There are two sandy beaches and a cove where all the boats are moored protecting them from the Nor Easters. Many families go back six and seven generations of Island residence.

Ruth's mother had babysat for a family when she was a teenager and fell in love with the Island. Later in 1940, a wealthy lady who liked her sold one of her houses completely furnished to her for twelve hundred dollars. Sixty years later, in 2000, the house would be appraised for almost half a million dollars. The house on Squirrel Island proved to be a wonderful place for our family to get together every summer. We keep a nineteen-foot outboard, *The Vet's Pet*, for frequent boat rides to Boothbay Harbor as well as other areas along the coast. There are many delightful spots to go out for meals by boat. The grandchildren also enjoy our small inflatable skiff with a three-horsepower outboard motor to tour around the cove. Squirrel is a very special spot where we all rest and reflect. A good portion of this book has been written while vacationing on Squirrel. Most of the cottages stay in the same families generation after generation.

Returning to the practice, I soon received the honor of being appointed to the Board of Examiners for Veterinary Medicine in New York State. I would serve on this board for the next ten years, and as the president of the board in 1982. This board governs the licensing procedures for the veterinary profession. Members of this board sit in judgment on all violations of the laws governing the practice of veterinary medicine in New York State. One of the major functions of the board at that time was the administration of the practical exam for licensure in the state. In addition to passing a national written test, all veterinarians seeking a license to practice the profession in New York State had to pass a hands-on exam using real animals. The exam was held twice a year at the New York State Veterinary College at Cornell. It was amazing to see some applicants who had completed four years of veterinary college somewhere in the world and still be unable to examine a real live horse, cow, or other animals.

One of the questions was to examine a cow for pregnancy. This required donning an arm-length plastic glove, inserting the arm in the cow's rectum, and palpating the uterus through the rectal wall. After several examinations, some of the cows started passing large amounts of gas. I remember one applicant, a gorgeous gal from the University of Pennsylvania with beautiful hair swept up on her head. During her exam, the cow passed a large amount of gas containing fecal matter that ended up on the side of her face and hair. While she was cleaning up, I asked her if she thought she would ever do the exam in her professional career. She looked at me and replied, "The only possibility is if I fail this exam and have to come back here again!" There was no way she would fail. She was brilliant. Eventually, the practical exam was eliminated, leaving only a written exam for licensure.

Administration of the practical exam for over ten years was an honor and allowed me to meet and become friends with many outstanding veterinarians from all over the state. Most of the male and female applicants taking the exam were extremely sharp. I found exposure to these brilliant minds that had just completed their educations tended to keep me updated on the latest advances in the profession.

One year I was rooming with Herb Bandameer, an outstanding veterinarian from Pittsford, New York. He had lost an eye and had received a prosthetic eye that looked almost normal. One morning before the exam I heard him starting to curse from our shared bathroom. While cleaning the glass eye, it had fallen down the drain in the lavatory. The exam was to start in less than an hour and Herb had a serious problem. After finally finding a pipe wrench, I took the trap apart under the sink and reunited Herb with his eye. After a quick cleaning and disinfecting, Herb was once again his handsome self and we made the exam just in time.

Herb, as well as all my professional colleagues, was shocked and saddened to learn of my later attempts at suicide. Although I suffered from depression the last few years on the board, I was able to function and I don't think any of my colleagues suspected my illness.

Back in Syracuse, the local SPCA shelter was getting some very adverse publicity. The Humane Association of Central New York started to publicly expose the plight of the animals staying at the Central New York SPCA shelter on Molloy Road in Syracuse. Conditions were deplorable. The shelter was poorly run with a totally inadequate staff. Cages were filthy and the shelter was definitely not living up to its name. The Board of Directors at the SPCA consisted of a very prominent group of businessmen in Syracuse and pressure was mounting on their leadership. One of the directors was a client and neighbor who felt they needed the help of a veterinarian. Quickly they elected Dave Taylor (a fellow veterinarian in North Syracuse) and me to their board. Since we knew about animal care, we were given a free hand to correct the shelter's problems. First we planned a complete renovation of their existing facility, installing stainless steel cages, which were much easier to clean and disinfect. Funds from various foundations were readily available to help make capital improvements. Next we designed a huge air-conditioned kennel building featuring large kennels with beds connecting to outside runs. The kennels and runs could be cleaned easily by hosing them down on a daily basis. I had designed this building on graph paper to scale right down to the last detail. The architect copied my drawing exactly and it was constructed for about one-hundred and fifty thousand dollars. The architect received eighteen thousand for supervising the construction. Dave and I didn't get a cent, but we had the satisfaction of designing a very useful building. The last improvement we were instrumental in constructing was an educational building, which has proved to be very valuable for use by the general public and many fundraising events. The combination of these improvements made a great turn-around for the image of the SPCA in Syracuse. Presently they have an excellent reputation and are the recipient of several bequests as animal-loving citizens pass on.

The other organization for animal welfare in Central New York is the Humane Association. Their first shelter was in the basement of my animal hospital in Fayetteville. Dolores Johnson was their first director and she was a very dear friend of every animal that was admitted. Later, as their organization grew, they opened a shelter in Liverpool. I made a strong attempt to merge the two organizations (SPCA and Humane Association). Despite several meetings and many advantages pointed out, the merger attempt failed. It was almost like merging the Democrats and Republicans—impossible.

The problem facing shelters today is the continuing overpopulation of cats and dogs. Despite many attempts to neuter pets, the problem still exists.

Unfortunately, many healthy young animals have to be put to sleep because of the overpopulation. Presently several shelters have adopted a *No Kill* policy, refusing to take in animals until space opens up after animals are adopted. This policy has resulted in animals being left to run wild, reproducing, and contributing to the overpopulation problem. No one likes to put perfectly healthy animals to sleep, but it is better than letting them run wild after meeting death from starvation, hit by cars, disease, or attacks from other animals.

Dave Taylor, my veterinarian colleague, formed *COPE* (Council on Pet Education) in the early 1970s. This organization was created to fight the overpopulation problem through educating the pet owners as to their responsibilities. Unfortunately, when Dave retired and moved to Colorado, the organization fizzled.

The most impressive attempt of our Veterinary profession to reduce the pet overpopulation problem has been made by a 1994 graduate of the New York State Veterinary College at Cornell.

Her name is Leslie Appel, DVM, and she has formed a nonprofit foundation called *Shelter Outreach Services*, or *SOS* for short. Presently she single-handedly neuters over one-hundred stray cats and dogs each week at ten county animal shelters in New York State. The counties she services are Tompkins, Cortland, Chenango, Schuyler, Seneca, Yates, Steuben, Tioga, Cayuga, and Onondaga. Ninety percent of the animals she neuters would never otherwise see a veterinarian for vaccinations and surgery.

My experience working with the SPCA opened my eyes to the multitude of foundations existing in this country eager to contribute to not-for-profit organizations involved in helping animals and/or disadvantaged citizens. Funds for capital improvements are readily available. Funds for operational expenses are much more difficult to obtain. Most foundations expect the recipient to be able to staff and maintain the capital improvements they pay for. This initiated the idea of forming my own foundation later in my life—*Jim Marshall Farms Foundation, Inc., where animals help people.*

As our children grew older and went off to college, we gave away the horses *Princess* and *Shadow* to neighbors. Our next project for the lamb house was raising pheasants. The state would provide the young chicks, which came in the mail. We would raise them up to a certain age and then just turn them loose in the woods behind our property. The cock pheasant is one of the most beautiful birds in America. I shot one once, had it mounted, and it still adorns our living room. Killing really bothers me and I quickly gave up hunting. I have no trouble eating pheasant, duck, venison, or other wildlife as long as someone else does the killing.

In 1973, I hired my first licensed animal technician, Niki James. She attended and graduated from the two-year course for AHTs at SUNY Delhi in New York. Nicky would prove to be a terrific addition to the practice. In my twenty-seven years of practice, I would have to rate her one of the best employees that have worked at Fayetteville Veterinary Hospital. Terry Drake and her mom, Nancy, are also among my favorite employees and still work for Dr. Chapman at the Vet Hospital.

In May of 1977, I embarked on a bold mission of construction on our Squirrel Island cottage in Maine. The house was badly in need of repair. It rested on a steep hill rising from the ocean. The front of the cottage had a huge amount of space underneath. The previous summer, I had taken measurements and designed on my trusted graph paper a complete living area under the existing house. This included four bedrooms, living room, kitchen, bath, front porch (overlooking the ocean), and a combination workshop and laundry area in the rear. The idea was to create an area our family of six could use without disturbing Ruth's mother and brother upstairs who were rather set in their ways.

After talking with some Maine builders who predicted a yearlong project, I decided to bring a crew from home that I had worked with previously constructing additions to the hospital. Earlier that winter and spring, I had accumulated beds, bedding, furniture, rugs, etc. to completely furnish the area once completed. We spent a lot of time watching the Pennysavers. The entire kitchen (consisting of kitchen cabinets, sink, counter, stove, and refrigerator) cost less than one-hundred dollars. All these items completely filled a large U-Haul van. I also purchased a used Boston Whaler with an outboard motor that we towed behind the U-Haul.

On May 14, 1977, I took off from home driving the U-Haul, boat, and trailer in tow with Vince Costello (one of the crew) to keep me company. Will Means, Barney Hagan, and John Havens went on ahead arriving in Boothbay Harbor before us. They holed up at the Thistle Inn where they immediately kept the bartender very busy. When I arrived in town, the police became very suspicious and pulled me over as we approached the Thistle Inn, which was our meeting place.

Vince jumped out of the moving van, ran into the Thistle Inn, and screamed to the rest of the crew, "The cops got Doc!" After I convinced the police that we were not going to blow up the town, we spent the night at the Cooper Inn. The next morning, I hired a large boat to take everything to the Island and launched the Boston Whaler. The project was underway.

Will Means was a terrific builder and most of the crew had worked for him previously. He took one look at the house and said, "Doc, I think you're crazy." Eventually I convinced him that this could be done and work began in earnest. We all stayed in the cottage, made our own breakfast, and ate lunch and dinner at the farmhouse on the Island. Everyone worked ten-to-twelve-hour days everyday, and in ten days, the project was complete. Completion of the project in ten days blew the minds of those who are used to moving at a much more relaxed pace. Twelve cases of beer had been consumed before the crew was paid and left for Central New York. That Memorial Day weekend we had a party celebrating the completion, plus my brother-in-law's birthday. It rained very heavily that night and mud from the construction was everywhere.

My one-hundred dollar kitchen stirred a great deal of controversy on Squirrel Island. Many residents thought two separate living quarters in one house was a terrible precedent. Many suspected that we would rent out the lower level to out-siders. It has never been occupied by anyone other than our family. I would rec-ommend this concept for any vacation cottage with a short summer season. This allows an entire family of four children and seven grandchildren to enjoy the beautiful Maine coast at the same time. Now that we're the senior citizens, we use the upper level and the noisy grandchildren are down below.

The Islanders have changed the rules so this can never happen again on Squir-rel Island. *NO second kitchen* is prominently listed in the rules. A better rule would be

Second kitchens or additional living quarters can only be used by the extended family in residence. Two cooks in one kitchen (even mother and daughter) often causes stress. This should be avoided—especially while on vacation.

In later years, we would add three more decks to the house. This construction led our family to give me the title *Doc Deck*. On a nice sunny summer day, you can always find a sunny or shady outside deck with a gorgeous view of the Atlan-tic Ocean.

The investment in the house on Squirrel Island has turned out to be one of my very best. The house has become the favorite vacation spot for all of our extended family and has definitely strengthened our family ties. The addition in 1977, plus the shed in back of the house allows us to sleep eighteen people, each with their own bed. We rarely reach capacity, but the cottage arrangement allows lots of our family to vacation at the same time without conflict.

My very favorite pastime at Squirrel is early morning tennis with a delightful group of elderly gentlemen. John Danforth is our leader and dictates all the rules. He won't divulge his age, but I am guessing that he is fifteen years my senior. (My next birthday is seventy.) Other regulars are Jack Lescure, Al Farrington, Jim Shepard, Richard Thomas, Admiral Bill Nivison, Ted Boyd, Steve Loro, Ed Ladendorff, and Reeves Morrison. Paul Tagliabue, the NFL commissioner also joins this group on occasion.

Recently I donated and constructed two *state of the art* horseshoe courts on the island. They both have extended platforms to accommodate female players as well. When we can no longer run around the tennis courts we can try horseshoes.

Returning to the practice in June of 1977, Kerry and Niki left to open their own hospital in Wampsville where Niki's family owned some land. To fill the void, I hired two new graduate veterinarians from Cornell: Dr. Ed Chapman and Dr. Fred Austin. Fred Austin only stayed a year or two. Ed, however, stayed for the next thirteen years and purchased the practice in April of 1990. In the early 1980s, when depression left me almost unable to function, Ed held the practice together. Although it would be a painful decision to sell the practice after building it from scratch, I was happy that Ed would be the one to take it over.

On September 13, 1977, my wonderful father passed away. He had suffered a stroke and was hospitalized in Syracuse. A few days before his death, he had pleaded with me to take him home. He even tried to call a taxi on his own. The doctors had convinced us that he was better off in the hospital. This has proven to be one of the biggest regrets of my life that we left him to die in the hospital. Most people, especially farmers, want to die at home with their family near them. I want all my heirs to know that I want to die at home when that time comes. My father was known and loved by most of Central New York. The turnout for his calling hours and funeral was tremendous.

The fall of 1977 marked the beginning of a twenty-three-year bout with depression. The winter blues were especially bad that fall, and for the first time, I asked Chuck Elliott, our friend and physician for help. He sent me to an elderly psychiatrist whom I liked very much. He was the only professional in my twenty-three-year bout with depression who asked me if I ever thought of harming myself (suicide). At that time, I had never thought that this could have entered my mind. I was blessed in so many ways with a wonderful wife, four great kids, a thriving practice, plenty of extended family support, membership in a country club, a beautiful vacation spot in Maine, and loads of friends. Everyone, including the doctors, my family, and myself included, thought this would be a temporary problem and I would soon snap out of it with the help of a little medicine. My only remaining parent had died, I was possibly burnt-out—it happens to a lot of professionals—and other explanations. However, I would continue to become more despondent and eventually suicidal in the next eight years. Full recovery would not occur until the year 2000—twenty-three years later. During this period, I would take twenty-five different antidepressant drugs, be hospitalized in four different hospitals, attempt suicide twice, and be seen by over a dozen psychiatrists or psychologists. Despite all this care, a brain tumor and a serious sleep disorder were overlooked.

It is very difficult to explain depressive illness to others that have never experienced this feeling. I know many people suffer from Migraine headaches that are severe in the disabling with out the pain. The difference is that the Migraine eventually goes away and you feel fine until the next one. With depression, the disability is constant with no relief, sometimes for years, seriously eroding ones confidence, happiness, potential, and even their ability to function. Thoughts of suicide eventually become a rational course of action to end ones agony.

My survival and recovery were miraculous! Many, many people suffer from this affliction to some extent at some point in their lives. I see symptoms in people almost every day. Perhaps my experience will help explain how devastating this illness can be. During my extended illness I never knew of anyone who survived. The main purpose of this book is to give those suffering hope for recovery. It may take years, but if I had a complete cure, so can you. If our country can spend eighty-three billion dollars to reconstruct Iraq, it certainly can invest more to find a cure for depression.

6

The 1980s

1980 in Syracuse marked the opening of the Carrier Dome. Ruth and I both love sports and we had been season ticket holders for both football and basketball from the opening until 2001. Attending the basketball games breaks up the long hard winters in Syracuse. Big East basketball and football are big time and are easy to get excited about. The Dome seats fifty thousand for football and has over thirty-three thousand for basketball, which is an on-campus record in the USA. We miss the old colorful coaches of the Big East: John Thompson of George-town, Rollie Massimino of Villanova, and especially Lou Carnesecca of St. John's. Even during my depressed years, I liked the games, but would feel so down and unable to get into the crowd frenzy of a close game. At these happy times, I would wonder, "Why do I feel so lousy???" Depression sucks!!!!

Regrettably in 2001 we cancelled our season tickets at the Carrier Dome. The University's lust for money became too much! No one can bring a snack to a game. Security removes any cookies or snacks that you have with you. The last straw for me came when our family attended a Princeton-Syracuse lacrosse game at the Dome. With forty thousand empty seats inside, security stopped my daughter-in-law carrying my nine-month-old grandson and made her buy a six-dollar ticket for the infant in her arms. This was the end for me!

The summer of 1980 proved to be the high point in my dismal golf career. I was fortunate to win a chance to play in the B.C. Open Pro-Amateur that is held the day before the tournament begins. The B.C. Open is held every year in Endi-cott, New York. The experience of the first tee with fans lined up on both sides of the tee was frightening. Fortunately, I hit the ball straight and avoided hitting anyone. We had four amateurs and one pro. Our pro was Dave Eichelberger who proved to be a great guy. Two of the amateurs were much better than I was, but the third was the County Executive for Broome County—a great guy but a terri-ble golfer. I was not the worst golfer in the group, which helped me relax. I even made a birdie on the second hole and beat the pro. The picture of our young family with Dave Eichelberger is one that I treasure.

That fall, Otey, our first-born, started his college career at Princeton University. He was an outstanding high school lacrosse player, which proved to be a plus along with a good scholastic record in gaining admission to this great Ivy League university. Otey made the varsity lacrosse team and became the first-string goalie in his junior and senior years. At that time, People's Airline had an extremely low fare to fly from Syracuse to Newark. Ruth and I took advantage of this and flew down to attend most of the home games. In one home game against Rutgers, Otey scored a goal, which is a very rare occurrence for a goalie. It was especially meaningful since Princeton won 14-13. We were so happy to have been there to witness that game.

Although I felt lousy most of the time, the practice ran smoothly thanks to the help of an excellent staff. Besides Ed Chapman, Dr. Florina Tseng joined our practice out of Cornell in 1982. Female vets were relatively new at that time and Flo was the first one in our practice. She proved to be a great veterinarian and the clients fell in love with her. She was from an outstanding Chinese family. All of her sisters and brothers were respected physicians.

Porge and Dick Chapman were directors of the horse show held every fall at the New York State Fair in Syracuse. They asked me to serve as one of the official veterinarians for the show. This was an enjoyable experience. I got to know some great people, including Deacon Doubleday, who was the announcer for the show for years. The *Speakin' Deacon* had a morning radio show from five to seven a.m. on WSYR. He was a favorite of dairy farmers during their morning milking session. Every barn radio was turned to the *Deacon*. Unfortunately, the Deacon was a chain smoker and his life was cut short as a result. His son, Peter, followed in his footsteps and presently is the announcer at several of the biggest shows in the country.

In later years, Harold and Rhea Ousby directed the horse show at the fair. They were good friends and clients, and also asked me to serve as the show vet. Their daughter, Naomi Bihuaniak, is a top horse show judge and attends many of the bigger shows in the country.

The practice was growing rapidly and kept us all very busy. Although the small animal hospital was by far the busiest and most lucrative, I never forgot about the farmers and their need for veterinary services. Occasionally, our integrity would be challenged. A cattle dealer called me one morning in early winter stating that one of his cows had drowned and he needed a veterinary statement for his insurance claim. When I arrived at the farm, I found a cow's body floating in the farm pond. It had been extremely cold the past few nights. The pond was frozen over and the body completely frozen. I wrote out a statement that the body was found in the pond, but due to the frozen condition I could not perform an autopsy to determine the cause of death. Apparently the insurance company paid the claim. A few weeks later the same client called with the same request for another cow that had drowned. When I arrived at the farm, I found evidence that the cow's dead body had been dragged out of the barn to the edge of the pond. The ice had been broken and the dead cow's head had been pushed under the water. He pushed a twenty-dollar bill in my pocket, explaining that the insurance company would never know the difference. I threw the twenty-dollar bill on the ground, left the farm, and told him never to call me again.

Jim Spear, our minister at the Fayetteville Methodist Church, was a good friend who spent many days trying to spark some life back into my morose existence. He would play tennis, basketball, take me boating, water skiing, together with spiritual counseling. This included a four-day religious retreat at Keuka College. Jim and I had played basketball against each other in high school. He played for Vernon High School and I played for Stockbridge Valley. In those days, the Vernon home games were played in a Town Hall gymnasium. The basket was nailed flush to the outside of the gym wall with chicken wire over the windows. There was a large round metal heat register in the center of the floor and the ceiling was only about fifteen feet high. A normal set shot would hit the ceiling and be declared out of bounds. These conditions took a while to adjust to and Vernon won most of their home games as a result. Jim was a good friend and my favorite minister. Unfortunately, cancer cut his life short—a great loss to me, as well as scores of other people.

In July of 1982, I met Vernon Snow, who headed up the John Ben Snow Foundation. Vernon was also a professor at Syracuse University and a decent tennis player. After our first breakfast meeting, he pledged twenty-five-thousand dollars to the SPCA renovation for two years in a row. John Ben Snow had made his fortune in the Woolworth Company and Vernon wrote an interesting biography of his life. The foundation he formed contributes generously to many worthwhile activities in Central New York, especially in the small village of Pulaski where John Ben Snow was born. In later years, Vernon encouraged me to form my own foundation using animals to help people and coached me on just how to go about it. Unfortunately, he did not live to see my dream fulfilled. He was definitely the one most responsible in making the Jim Marshall Farms Foundation, Inc. a reality.

My depression was gradually worsening and visits to the psychiatrist were more frequent. I can vividly remember driving into Syracuse on Route 690 looking at the State Tower building and wondering why I wasn't getting better. The visits were expensive and weren't covered by insurance. It seemed that each visit involved trying a new drug or a change in dosage, always with no improvement. The biggest problem was insomnia, which is often associated with depression. Friends of mine from college days couldn't believe that Jim Marshall could ever have a problem sleeping. In those days, I could fall asleep at the drop of a hat and often in the middle of a lecture. One of the drugs prescribed for my sleep problem was Dalmane. The psychiatrist informed me that I could take this drug as needed for long periods. I took Dalmane for years. Later I would learn that Dalmane should only be taken for three-week periods. Prolonged use can cause insomnia rather than treat it. This may have contributed to my downfall. Throughout my illness, I never took any drug without a prescription from a physician.

The 1980s would prove to be the worst decade of my life. My visits to psychologists and psychiatrists became more frequent and more disappointing and frustrating. The depression did not get better—it got worse! Despite the medication, the psychotherapy, and the family support, I gradually lost my zest for life, my ability to be creative, and worst of all my interest in working in the wonderful profession of veterinary medicine. I was able to function—take office calls, perform surgery, and fool a lot of clients and friends that I was okay. My biggest regret was missing out on those wonderful years when the kids were young, growing up, and in need of parental guidance and companionship. When I got home, I would collapse on the couch or stay in bed. Ruth was left with pretty much all the responsibility of raising the kids and caring for the house and meals—all this plus a morose husband who did not help out much and gradually got worse and worse. I could fool the clients, but my entire family knew that I was a sick puppy. I provided plenty of financial support for the family, but that was about all. Unfortunately, our children have memories of a despondent father lying in bed or on the couch—no fun at all. Without a stay-at-home mom who guided the kids through those terrible years, we all may have failed!

Unfortunately, all this time a tumor was growing on my pituitary gland at the base of my brain, which I would not discover until 1987. I firmly believe that depression adversely affects one's immunity and the ability to fight off illness, including tumors and cancer. Anyone suffering from any mental illness should have a brain scan to rule out a possible physical cause. In my case, an earlier diagnosis could have prevented my downward spiral to suicide in 1985.

My Uncle Fred's death in September of 1982 added to my grief. He was ninety-one years of age and the last of that wonderful generation on my father's side of the family. I'm glad that my wonderful parents and Uncle Fred did not live to witness my deterioration to suicide attempts. Children often present problems for their parents, but there can be nothing worse than losing a child to suicide.

Few people understand the devastating effect depression and suicide have on the immediate family. Fortunately, in my case, our family stayed together, the kids all went to college and turned out fine.

To help you grasp the extent of the problem of suicides among the younger segment of our population, I would like you to read excerpts from an article entitled, "*The Growing Problem of Youth Suicide*" by Senator Susan Collins of Maine that appeared in the Boothbay Harbor Register during the summer of 2001.

"*The growing national problem of youth suicide is often a topic that is brushed under the rug because it is such a difficult subject to broach. Talk about it we must because, tragically, suicide rates among American young people have increased dramatically in recent years, and in Maine, the rate is higher than the national average.*

...the incidence of suicide among adolescents and young adults had tripled over the last 45 years even though suicide rates among the general population have remained fairly stable. More teenagers and young people die from suicide than from cancer, heart disease, AIDS, birth defects, stroke, pneumonia, influenza, and chronic lung disease combined.

There currently are about 5,000 teen suicides each year, and suicide is the third leading cause of death among young people, following unintentional injuries and homicide. Moreover, it is the second cause of death among our college students. According to the National College Health Risk Behavior Survey conducted by the Centers for Disease Control and Prevention (CDC), one in ten college students had seriously considered suicide during the previous year, and most had gone so far as to draw up a plan.

The statistics are even more worrying, however, for high school students. According to the CDC Youth Risk Behavior Survey, one out of five high school students nationwide had seriously considered suicide during the preceding year.....Moreover, 10 percent of our (Maine) female students actually made an attempt, and three percent of the high school students made an attempt that was serious enough to require medical attention."

The governor of Maine at that time, Governor King, appointed a task force to develop a comprehensive plan to prevent youth suicide. They soon learned that no single strategy can work to prevent youth suicide. The approach must be multi-faceted. This is also the same goal of the U.S. Surgeon General in working on the national level.

Senator Collins concludes by saying that *"suicide prevention...requires a concerted effort among a coalition of parents, teachers, students, health care workers, and government officials if it is to be effective."*

Additionally, depression and suicide often take over the lives of our most talented and gifted young people. An article that appeared in *People* magazine on December 17, 2001 describes the tragic circumstances of several students who committed suicide at Massachusetts Institute of Technology (MIT), the elite institution in Cambridge, Mass. In fact, between 1990 and 2001 eleven MIT students took their own lives, contributing to what some experts have described as a decade-long contagion of self-destruction. Since 1990, students at MIT have been three times more likely to kill themselves than those at other colleges.

The article states that *"There are no easy explanations for the phenomenon, and the students had little in common with one another. But Madelyn Gould, a Columbia University psychiatrist who had researched suicide clusters, says that when a troubled youth learns that others have killed themselves, it makes suicide seem like a more viable option to end his or her own pain."*

Recent tragedies at MIT leave little doubt that helping students in crisis can be an exceedingly complex challenge with life-and-death consequences.

It seems that every month there are articles in newspapers all over the country about the tragic relationship between depression and the often-resultant suicides that occur. There is a definite need for help for these desperate people of all ages.

7

Those Wonderful Standardbred Horses

About the only bright spot in the decade of the 1980s was the introduction of the Standardbred and harness racing into my morbid existence. Early in the spring of 1983, a client invited me out to the farm on which he was working for a wealthy owner. He harnessed up a racehorse and had me jog the horse around the farm-training track. It was a beautiful spring morning, the sun was just coming up, the birds were singing, and I immediately knew what I wanted to do with the rest of my life. I fell in love with the Standardbred and harness racing.

Soon after this experience, I bought a one-third interest in my first horse together with my friend, George Soufleris, and the trainer Bud Wahl. His name was *Ingredient* and he was a loser! Never made it to the races, and therefore, never made a dime.

I was hooked, however, and later that spring I found myself at an auction of horses at the Meadowlands in New Jersey. A striking two-year-old entered the ring and I just had to own that horse! When the hammer fell, I had purchased my first horse for $19,500. I never paid this much for a horse since that day, and I have bought a lot of them.

His name was *National Star*. He was not a loser and turned out to be a very dear friend of mine. Horses are just like people. Some you just love and turn out to be friends for life. Others just don't impress you and turn out to be just another horse with no special bond. *Star* was not especially gifted, rather bad gaited, but had tremendous desire. He beat a lot of better horses because of this desire. Later in his life as a stallion, he passed this desire to his offspring. Presently I have his grandson, *JMF's Sam*, who is now twelve years old, has made over $125,000, and is still racing with the same great desire.

When I came to my senses, I realized that financially I was in over my head. A partnership was formed and four of my friends agreed to put ten thousand dollars each into the venture. One of the partners paid his share in a different way. One day I was working in the hospital when one of our gals told me that a man in a pick-up truck was parked in front of the garage for a long time. When she asked him if she could help, he asked her if I could come out to the truck. When I went out, my future partner presented me with a paper bag containing ten thousand dollars, all in small bills—five, ten, and twenty dollar bills. This was more cash than I had ever seen in my life. What do you do with all this cash?? I soon found out that you don't just walk into a bank with this much cash without raising some eyebrows. Finally I convinced him to come back, pick up the cash, and give me a check for ten thousand dollars.

The partnership worked out fairly well. My mental health was deteriorating with the depression, and I decided to terminate the partnership in October of 1985 and paid everyone off. Two of the partners decided to continue on with *National Star* and they made money as a result. Saying goodbye to this great horse was painful. Fate, however, would reunite us a few years later.

My love affair with the Standardbred was serious and soon I was looking for a farm to buy. My first interest was the farm in North Chittenango where *National Star* was stabled. It had a real nice one-half mile training track, but most of the farm was in a flood plain and flooded badly every spring. When negotiations to buy this farm broke down, I learned of another farm also in North Chittenango. This was a much better value with three barns and a nice old farmhouse covering 213 acres. The farm was owned by old clients of mine (Don and Florence Taylor) and negotiations went smoothly.

The only drawback compared to the first farm was the lack of a training track. There was, however, a beautiful field, very flat, where a five-eighths-mile track could be constructed. I had to build a racetrack, but a five-eighths-mile track is superior to a half-mile track.

The farm purchase was completed in July of 1984—*Jim Marshall Farms* was born. In no time, I had surveyed and located where the five-eighths-mile track and main stable would be located. Clint Getty, a surveyor, helped me with the survey. Clint is a great guy. (If you remember, he was the owner of the famous *Puddy Cat* that escaped from my hospital a few years earlier.) The five-eighths-mile track fit perfectly in an open field and was located six-hundred feet back from New Boston Road. It had a natural hedge row on the eastern, western, and southern border of the farm and the trains were clearly visible from the main stable. Specifications for the construction of a five-eighths-mile track were available from the United States Trotting Association and the track was constructed exactly as specified. The wide gradual turns of the larger tracks (five-eighths, seven-eighths, and one mile) are much easier on the horses' legs.

Figuring out the drainage and construction of this large track was quite an engineering challenge for a veterinarian. Although the field appeared perfectly flat, there was a six-foot difference from one side to the other. We had to excavate three feet from the high side and fill the three feet on the lower side. First the top soil (one foot deep) had to be pushed to the outside. This mound of top soil would eventually form the base of the *people track* that would later be constructed as a walking/jogging track surrounding the horse-training track. During this construction, I purchased an old John Deere backhoe-loader on rubber tires. I learned rather quickly how to operate the backhoe. Two levers controlled the operation of the backhoe, each moving in four directions. After enough experience, you learn to move these levers without even thinking about what each movement does. (Just like playing the piano!) Operating this old backhoe myself not only saved me a fortune (hiring a backhoe is seventy-five to one-hundred dollars per hour), but also became my favorite therapy for depression. Digging a drainage ditch with the backhoe became my favorite pastime.

I also purchased an old bulldozer, an old 656 International tractor, an old Allis Chalmers WD-40 tractor, a brand new hydraulic dump wagon, and a new post-hole digger. It is now twenty years later. All of this equipment still works and running these antiques is still my favorite pastime. It's just like playing in the sandbox, but with bigger toys.

To fill the lower side of the track, we had to dig a large pond in the infield of the track (three hundred feet by fifty feet) and another pond on the southeast outside edge of the track (heart-shaped, one hundred and fifty feet across—later to be called Sweetheart Pond). The pond in the infield would later be used for swimming horses. The drainage was directed to the pond in the infield, which overflowed into the heart-shaped pond and then off the property to the east. This was such a large area that every time it rained, the ponds were both filled to the top.

The Kinsella family, who owned a quarry on the western border of my veterinary hospital location, was extremely helpful building the track. On several weekends in the summer of 1984, they would bring heavy equipment to the farm and eventually constructed the track. I paid the men in cash and had plenty of beer and pizza available for them at the end of the hot and dusty days. The men liked the extra cash, and since the equipment wasn't used in the quarry on weekends, I was able to build a terrific track for a fraction of the normal cost. As a result, we have one of the finest farm training tracks in Central New York. The Kinsellas have been terrific neighbors and friends for over forty years. I could never have developed the farm without their help.

Next, the main stable was constructed right in front of the finish line of the track. The building was built by the Brescia Pole Barn Company that builds nothing but horse barns. I wanted a lounge and office upstairs so the barn was built with two stories. The ground floor includes nine stalls, a bathroom, and a wash stall. The second floor had the lounge, a small kitchen, a bath with shower, and a large area for hay storage. We built a large deck off the lounge, which proved to be a delightful spot overlooking the track and unspoiled countryside. The lounge and deck were built by my son Otey and his friend Craig Putnam. This was done during his summer vacation from Princeton. I also built seven shelters and fourteen paddocks with water and electricity supplied to each shelter. During the many years of depression, I would sit on this deck, all by myself, in the evenings until darkness. The peaceful setting, watching the mares and their foals in the infield, the beautiful countryside, an occasional train going by, and the setting sun was truly therapeutic. I knew then that if I could survive my illness, I would attempt to make this peaceful setting available to others suffering with depression or any other problems life brings to us. This is really where and when the idea of a foundation that brought animals together with people was born.

When the barn was completed, I needed more horses. *National Star* was, of course, the first horse in the barn. Since I wanted more horses like *Star*, he had to have some wives. Soon I was back at the auction barn in New Jersey looking for mares due to have babies in the spring. The first mare in the sale was *Bewitching Lobell* in foal to *Temurjen*. I was able to buy her cheap at fifteen hundred dollars. For the next two hours, some guy kept coming up to me, trying to buy her, each time with a higher offer. When I was ready to go, he offered me twenty-five hundred dollars. I could have made a thousand dollar profit without getting out of my chair, but I turned it down. A little later in the sale I bought *Raspberry*, who was in foal to *Brand New Fella*. I had two nice wives for *National Star* and would have two babies in the spring.

Depression was really getting worse and worse. Visits to the professionals were longer, more frequent, involved more drugs with increased dosage, and unfortunately, absolutely no improvement was happening. I was working as hard as I possibly could with the practice and the farm, constantly exhausted (mentally and physically), and had more and more problems with insomnia. It is hell to be so exhausted and not be able to sleep. I was taking a lot of Dalmane and other sleep medication, always as directed by a physician. Later I would discover this was a big mistake.

For some reason, I thought that bow hunting would be a healthy diversion for the fall season in 1984. I knew I couldn't shoot a deer with a gun, but thought bow hunting would be different. It wasn't. After completing an archery course, purchasing all the equipment, complete with a camouflage suit, and constructing a tree stand behind the house, I was ready. The location of the tree stand is the key. You have to study the trails in the woods and try to determine when the deer use the trails—the more frequent the better! To find this out, I tied thread across the trails and checked them as often as possible to monitor the deer activity. Finally, I found the perfect spot and built my tree stand.

The first day of bow hunting season, I was up in the tree stand with all my equipment, my quiver filled with arrows (with nasty razor-sharp tips), the morning paper, and a nice thermos of coffee. It was absolutely beautiful up there. The leaves were pretty much off the trees and I could see and hear the different sounds of the many animals in the woods. Before long, a beautiful doe with her two fawns appeared and all three stopped right under my tree stand. I could almost reach down and pet them. Although legally I could shoot a doe, the thought of those nasty, cutting arrows plunging through that beautiful skin and breaking up that nice family was too much. I couldn't shoot the bow either! I did return several more mornings to the tree stand. I read the paper, drank my coffee, and enjoyed the beauty of the woods. I didn't bother to bring the bow and arrows—I knew I couldn't use them.

8

Those Horrible Suicidal Thoughts

The worst year of my life was by far 1985. The prolonged depression was taking its toll. I was having difficulty functioning in a normal manner. A tremor developed in my hands and performing surgery became more difficult. I even had the technicians help me with threading the needles and suturing the skin. The simple routine surgeries, like spaying a cat or dog, became a real challenge.

Up until 1985, I had never even thought of ending my suffering by my own intent. The first psychiatrist I saw back in 1977 asked me if I ever thought of ending my life. I honestly answered at that time that the thought never entered my mind. I was blessed in so many ways with a wonderful family, thriving practice, and loads of good friends. How could anyone possibly think of suicide? Oddly enough, although I saw at least a dozen mental health professionals over the next eight years, no one ever asked me if I had ever considered suicide. I think this is a big mistake. A very high percentage of people with depression develop a secret wish for suicide as the terminal cure of their suffering. This factor should definitely be thoroughly discussed in the doctor-patient relationship.

Depression often continues on for months and years. It is not like a bad cold that lasts three weeks or a broken bone that takes six to eight weeks to completely heal. There comes a time in the course of depressive illness when the patient needs to be hospitalized to avoid attempts at suicide. Not only the professional, but also friends and family members should take action to admit the depressed individual before it is too late. Suicide is often predictable. No one has the strength and fortitude to resist the secret wish to end their suffering forever. Almost everyone can become suicidal as a result of prolonged suffering when hope for recovery vanishes. If it happened to me, it can happen to you.

In a recent article, Surgeon General David Satcher said, "There are few who escape being touched by the tragedy of suicide in their lifetimes." He added that suicide is the eighth leading cause of death in the United States, killing over thirty thousand people each year. More than six hundred and fifty thousand people make the attempt. In an article by Senator Susan Collins of Maine (printed earlier in this book), she states that one out of every four of the teenagers in the state of Maine have seriously considered suicide at one time in their young lives. If this is the case in the wonderful laid-back population of Maine, I'm sure that similar statistics can be found throughout the country. This adds up to millions of our young people who are finding the problems of life overwhelming and seriously consider ending the wonderful God-given gift of life. This illness is not a small problem for America or the rest of the world.

In my own opinion, there are two major reasons why people with depressive illness attempt suicide.

The first factor is the failure to get better over a long period of time, often even with the help of professional therapy and medication. The thought of spending the rest of one's life this way is a catalyst. In my own life, the downward spiral with no improvement over eight years was the main reason. Despite seeing the very best professionals and taking over twenty-five different medications from 1977 to 1985, I just got worse and worse. My recovery became hopeless.

The second factor causing suicide is the fear of being incarcerated in mental hospitals for the rest of your life. Once you enter the system of hospitalization, the opportunity to end your suffering is gone. I have been a patient in three mental hospitals in my life, and believe me, there is no opportunity to hurt yourself. All the doors are locked, bars over the windows, absolutely no glass or sharp objects, and constant around-the-clock vigilance by personnel. Once you get out of these facilities, you never want to go back. They are not happy places. There is a very high risk of repeated suicide attempts, especially in patients who don't fully recover from their depressive illness. I know the hospitals could be improved. The thought of having to return to one of these dreadful lock-ups often pushes these people over the edge and they choose suicide instead.

It was my observation that the main emphasis in these hospitals is preventing the patients from hurting themselves. Of course, they would face a large lawsuit if this happens. Very little is done to convince the patients to recognize the incredible value of the God-given gift of life. Most of these patients have been suffering for months and years. They are convinced that they are never going to get better. They have talked and talked (and given a good portion of their life savings) to psychiatrists and psychologists. Often their illness has led to rejection from friends, family, and even organized religion. Their self-esteem is at an all-time low.

I never once met anyone during my hospital days who had made a full recovery and enjoyed life again. These patients need to talk with former patients who have recovered.

In my own case, the illness covered a span of twenty-three years before I could say I was fully recovered. It is very hard to maintain a hope for recovery and future happiness during these long periods of illness. I hope every patient in mental care facilities can read this book and be convinced to never, never give up hope for a full recovery.

Following my first suicide attempt, which was well known in Fayetteville, Vernon Lee, our wonderful Methodist minister, came to visit me in the hospital. Following communion and prayer, I asked him as he was about to leave, "Vernon, I don't know how I can go back to my clients, my family, my friends, and the community after attempting suicide. Do you know anyone who has done this and made it back?" After a long pause, he replied, "Why, no, I don't know of anyone who has." At that moment of deep, deep despair, I vowed to God that if I could ever make it back and recover, I would be willing to answer anyone's call for help—anytime—anywhere.

Now that the *Jim Marshall Farms Foundation, Inc.* is approved and functioning, I hope to have a place for people with suicidal thoughts to visit to give them hope that they too can recover. First, I want them to read this book and realize the personal struggle I lived through which led me to develop the farm facility and the foundation. As they are exposed to the animals, the miracle of life (newborn animals), the beautiful rural environment, the support of scores of *JMF Boosters*, the *Canine Consultants* and the personal counseling of the *Life Mentors*, I am sure that they will be convinced to cling to the wonderful God-given gift of life and fight off the Satan-driven wish for death.

Early in 1985, the thoughts of ending my suffering started to invade my thoughts. The continuing disappointments of the professional visits (constantly changing medications and dosages) tended to reinforce the recourse of suicide.

As a youngster, I was fortunate to have a wonderful uncle (the husband of my mother's sister). They had no children of their own and welcomed the frequent visits of my sister Zoe and myself when we were very young. Uncle Lee had a wonderful sense of humor and thoroughly enjoyed our visits. The happy memories of playing croquet in their backyard in Elmira are vivid. I'm not sure of all the facts in the deterioration of his mental health. No one seemed to tell us much except that Uncle Lee was sick. I can remember seeing him at family reunions—completely morose showing no interest in his nieces and nephews. This seemed like a very strange illness to all of us at that time. Now, after surviving all these years, I know he was suffering from severe depression. Unfortunately, he never realized any improvement that I know of. Eventually he ended up in a state mental hospital, which was a fate worse than death. His wife, my Aunt Zoe, was a wonderful person, strong and resilient in character. She took charge of all his business ventures, which were failing, worked hard as a schoolteacher and paid off all of Uncle Lee's debts. Bankruptcy would have been a much easier financial route to take, but she was too proud for that. Aunt Zoe and I had the same birthday (November fourth). This kept us very close over the years. One year I acquired a young filly to settle a bad debt. Before a horse races, for twenty-five dollars, you can change the name of the horse, so I named the filly *My Aunt Zoe.* That same fall, the filly won a big race at the Syracuse Mile. The newspaper in Elmira discovered the name connection and selected Aunt Zoe as the ninety-year-old Athletic "Star" of the week in Elmira. The notoriety was tremendous and she enjoyed every minute of it.

I last visited Aunt Zoe with my daughter Jennifer and granddaughter, Sarah, Monday, December 6, 1999. She was ninety-six years old, mentally sharp, and as always vivacious. Two days later she had a massive heart attack and died. Our world had lost a very great lady! She was a role model for all of us. Live as long as you possibly can, help others all you possibly can, and die quickly. We all were happy that Aunt Zoe never had to linger in a nursing home. She took care of herself in her own house in her own way for ninety-six years, right up to the moment of her death. I hope and pray I can do the same!

As 1985 dragged on, the combination of the failure to see any improvement from doctors and medication, and the memory of Uncle Lee's fate, led me to seriously consider suicide. Eventually it led to not whether I would end my life, but when.

I am very bitter that none of the professionals I was seeing that year thought to have a brain scan done. If they had ordered a scan, the slow-growing brain tumor would have been discovered. This would have given me an explanation as to why the depression would not improve and hope for possible recovery. The revelation of the tumor would have removed those terrible thoughts of suicide.

Around Labor Day of 1985, I removed the .357 Magnum revolver, plus one .38 mm bullet from the safe. The revolver had remained in the safe unused for over twenty-three years, ever since I returned from Connecticut and built the hospital. This revolver had the reputation of being so powerful that a slug would pass through the block of a car engine. I knew that one shot to the head would end my suffering forever.

Once this secret plan was adopted, it then became a question of when. For months, the loaded gun remained hidden under the seat of my practice van. Several times I drove deep into remote country roads, and each time lost my nerve to perform the execution. I firmly believed that Satan was taking over my life and all hope of recovery was gone. I continued to see the professionals on regular visits. They never inquired about suicidal plans and I never revealed the secret wish to end my suffering. I kept hoping the next visit would be different, however, nothing changed.

I'm convinced that most successful suicides occur in this manner, and gunshots are by far the most effective choice. People don't just decide to end their life after a few days of despair. Some try to seek sympathy and make half-hearted attempts to hurt themselves. However, when someone puts a gun to their head (as I did), or hooks an exhaust hose up to the inside of a car (as Dr. Delahanty did), they are not looking for sympathy. They definitely want to end their suffering forever.

September 10, 1985 marked my last meeting as President of the State Board for Veterinary Medicine in New York State. I was awarded a plaque recognizing my contribution to this great profession as President of the Board of Examiners—truly a great honor in our profession. Following the meeting in Albany, Ruth and I traveled up to Squirrel Island to close up the cottage for the season. Serious thoughts of driving the boat way out in the ocean and making my suicide look like a boating accident raced through my sick brain. A few days at Squirrel always had the effect of raising my spirits and hope for recovery, but not on this trip. Doom and gloom prevailed.

On November 9, 1985, Cynthia and Sam announced their engagement to be married at a party at our house. It was a happy occasion for everyone but me. I was struggling to try and act normal in front of our close friends, relations, and guests. Looking back at the family pictures taken that night, it was obvious that I was a sick puppy. I knew that my remaining days on earth were numbered. The end was near.

9

Friday the 13th

I had decided that December 13, 1985, would be the last day of my life on planet Earth. My last note to Ruth and the family was written and placed in an envelope along with several thousand dollars in cash. I knew she would need this money to care for the house and family until my will would distribute my assets. The note stated how much I loved Ruth and the kids, and how I thought ending my suffering would be the best solution for everyone. Financially they all would be in good shape. The downward spiral since 1977 had convinced me that improvement was impossible and the rest of my life in a mental hospital draining our life savings was not going to happen. Suicide was the solution and the loaded .357 Magnum would get the job done.

I went to the hospital, saw several office calls, and had one piece of surgery to do—a cat spay. The tremor in my hands was worse than ever and the technician's concern was obvious. She kept asking me if I was feeling okay. I lied, telling her the tremor was due to too much coffee, when I hadn't had a drop. The technician had to suture the wound. I was much too shaky to accomplish this simple task. I can't remember if I had any lunch that day, but I do remember leaving the hospital around four in the afternoon.

Ruth and I were invited to a Christmas cocktail party at a friend's house, scheduled to start at six at night. Facing friends and clients in my condition was impossible. Without saying a final goodbye to anyone at home, I left the envelope (with the note and cash) on my desk, started our Dodge Omni with the .357 Magnum under my seat, and left home on what was planned to be my last trip.

For some time I had planned to end my life over the graves of my mother and father who were buried in the Stockbridge cemetery. Of all the possible locations to end my life, this seemed to be number one. I guess I wanted to be as close as possible to Mom and Dad when my life ended.

As I left Fayetteville on Route 5, it started snowing really hard, so hard that at times it was hard to see the road. When I arrived at the cemetery in Stockbridge, the Dodge Omni would not go up the steep driveway leading to the section of the cemetery where Mom and Dad were buried side by side. After the second try, I knew I couldn't make it. There was no flashlight in the car and finding my way to the graves in the dark during a bad snowstorm would be impossible.

My second choice of location was outside the bedroom of the family homestead where I was born. This was only a few miles to the south on the Pratts Hollow Road. I kept driving up and down the road past our homestead from Munnsville to Pratts Hollow and back again, delaying the execution as long as possible. Finally, I stopped in front of a phone booth in Munnsville for a long time thinking about calling Ruth or the psychologist.

Miraculously my brother Tom drove by, recognized the Dodge Omni, and stopped. By this time, Ruth had read the suicide note and called all the relatives and State Troopers. Tom invited me back to the homestead where I parked the Omni in the machinery shed and entered the home where I was born and grew up to college age.

My sister, Ada May, and her husband, Bob, soon arrived and everyone tried their best to cheer me up, explaining all the ways that my life was blessed. Ada May read a letter that our Dad had sent her in her college days, but my despondent state of mind was impervious to any positive reasoning. After several phone calls to Ruth and the medical people, it was decided that I would stay at Tom's and go on to the mental hospital in the morning.

The guestroom in the homestead was our parents' bedroom when we were growing up. It was the same room that I was born in, as well as my older brother, Fred, and sisters, Ada May and Zoe Mary. By the time my younger brother Tom was born, all births were attended at the Oneida City Hospital.

Now the cycle of my life would be complete. I would be ending my life in the very same room that I was born in fifty-two years earlier. The entire night was spent with the .357 Magnum positioned against my head waiting for the moment that I would pull the trigger. The revolver had the capacity for six shells (a six shooter) and I had no idea when the one fatal shell would rotate into position. Over a period of several hours, I pulled the trigger three times, only to hear a resounding click. My right hand holding the revolver against my temple became tired, so I laid the gun against my throat, pointing upwards against my chin.

The fourth sound was not a click. It was the loudest sound I have ever heard in my life. I was supposed to be dead, but I wasn't. Blood was gushing out of a wound in my neck making a mess of the bed. Immediately I wished I had more bullets to finish the job—I wanted to die in the worst way. The bullet had entered the right side of my neck under my chin and exited just behind my left ear. The odds of surviving a gunshot of this magnitude are more than one in a million. I firmly believe to this day that God pushed Satan aside and saved my life. Obviously he had a plan for my life here on earth.

When one considers all the vital anatomy in this part of our bodies, it seems only more miraculous that I survived. The bullet avoided the spinal cord, spine, carotid arteries, vagus nerves, jugular veins, trachea, larynx, epiglottis, esophagus, ear canal, and base of the brain.

The gunshot woke everyone in the house and soon the ambulance arrived and backed right up to the front door of the homestead. In a small rural community like Munnsville, the volunteer fire company serves as the ambulance service. The attendant in the ambulance was Marie Mason, a nice gal I went to high school with thirty-four years earlier. I was considered one of the more successful graduates of Stockbridge Valley Central and I'm sure Marie, as well as everyone else in town, wondered why in the world I would attempt to end my very successful life. Success does not make anyone immune from depression!

The ambulance took me to the Oneida City Hospital emergency room in Oneida. Once the doctor was satisfied that my medical condition was stable, a State Trooper entered the room and questioned me at length about the shooting. Once he was convinced that I indeed was the only one involved—obviously a suicide attempt—he left the room.

Shortly thereafter, Ruth and the kids arrived at the hospital. Everyone except me seemed to be genuinely happy that I was still alive. The gunshot did not help my depression, which would continue in my life for the next fourteen years. [I still wanted to be dead ending my suffering.] A second attempt to end my life was in the near future.

Ruth insisted that I be moved to a Syracuse hospital where our good friend, Dr. Bill Stewart, would monitor my care. Bill is the neurosurgeon that operated on Brother Fred several times, first removing his large brain tumor and later correcting the many complications that followed the original surgery. Bill suggested the Crouse Irving Memorial Hospital in Syracuse. I was moved immediately to the Intensive Care Unit by ambulance.

I can still remember vividly Bill's examination of all the functions that could have been destroyed or impaired by the shot. Both Bill and the ENT doctor (Dr. Doug Halliday) were amazed at how I could have survived a gunshot in this location of the body. Dr. Halliday did the surgery to clean the path of the bullet through my neck. This required a tracheotomy through which I would breathe for the next two weeks while the surgical site was healing. The scars are vivid reminders of this ordeal that I get to view everyday while shaving.

Since Crouse Irving Memorial Hospital did not have a psych ward, I had to stay in the Intensive Care Unit, which provided the most constant surveillance of any area in the hospital. I was about as popular as a turd in a flower shop. Here I was in an environment with critically ill patients who were fighting to survive. My physical health was excellent, but mentally I wanted to die. Most of the nurses displayed an obvious dislike for my presence. I had a curtain pulled around my bed at all times keeping me isolated from view. One day a book dropped on the floor from my bedside table making a loud noise. A nurse ripped open the curtain expecting to witness another suicide attempt. The disgusted look on her face is etched forever in my memory. Actually I needed very little care. The surgical wound in my neck healed perfectly. There was one nurse who had a great deal of compassion for my illness. I think she knew of my professional reputation in Syracuse and would stop by my bedside when she had time with kind words of encouragement. I can't remember her name, but I hope someday she hears about this book, my ultimate recovery, the foundation, and introduces herself so I can properly thank her in person for her compassion during those very dark days of my life.

The psychologist that I had been seeing prior to the suicide attempt visited me a few times and was in charge of my care. I think I probably was the first suicidal patient he had ever seen. He obviously missed the boat in failing to hospitalize me before my first suicide attempt and I feel he was also directly negligent in allowing my second suicide attempt to happen while under his care, which will be explained shortly. Until my dying day, I will hold this individual responsible for both my suicide attempts. In spite of his obvious negligence, he still had the nerve to send me a bill of seven hundred dollars for his medical care while I was hospitalized, which was not covered by insurance. Some doctors' lust for money is beyond belief! I hope this experience helped him identify suicidal potential in future patients before it was too late for them. I'm sure he didn't feel too good about the result of his care of me, but a simple get-well wish or note of compassion would have helped my forgiveness of his negligence.

One thing I did find out from another psychiatrist at the hospital was that my previous use of the drug Dalmane was definitely wrong. He explained that Dalmane should only be taken for a maximum of three weeks. I had taken it regularly for several years as a sleep aid. This prolonged misuse of this potent drug very well could have contributed to my suicidal state of mind. Originally a psychiatrist prescribed Dalmane for my insomnia and told me I could take it every evening as long as I had a problem sleeping, which was every night. Every doctor I saw, I informed of my use of all drugs including Dalmane. No one informed me of the danger that this drug creates with prolonged use.

Since therapeutic drugs are such a major part in the treatment of all forms of mental illness, seeing a psychiatrist who is an MD, educated, and trained in the indication, proper dosage, side effects, and capable of prescribing a multitude of available drugs is a necessity. Psychologists do not have this necessary training, and therefore, cannot prescribe and monitor the effects of the drugs for mental illness. Often it seems to be a trial-and-error process of treating patients. What works well on one person may not help the next patient. In my own struggle over twenty-three years, I counted twenty-five different drugs that were prescribed and consumed at one time or another. None of the drugs seemed to alter my constant downward progression of this terrible illness.

My suicidal state of mind did not change at Crouse. I still wanted to die and every day brought more thoughts of how I could end my suffering. The shower stall I was permitted to use had an emergency cord one could pull for help. Thoughts of how I could use this cord to hang myself consumed my imagination. This proved to be impossible. I'm always amazed when I hear of prisoners that successfully commit suicide in a jail cell using bed sheets, shoe laces, etc. These individuals must have a great deal of ingenuity. If they could ever be cured, they would succeed as engineers, inventors, or in other vocations requiring creative abilities. History has proven that creative, ingenious individuals are prone to mental illness, especially depression, and the resulting thoughts of suicide. For years this illness has been hushed up, avoiding publicity and considered a personal weakness no one wanted to reveal. Today prominent, successful individuals in our society have revealed mental illness in their own lives (Mike Wallace, Art Buchwald, Winston Churchill, and many others). This publicity, along with the giant strides in better drugs will help save a lot of lives.

Christmas 1985 was the worst Christmas in my life. Due to my unstable condition, I was not allowed to leave the hospital. Ruth brought all the kids into the hospital, along with presents for everyone. The prospect of returning home someday to enjoy Christmas with the family in our home together with the tree, Christmas decorations, the big meal with both fireplaces burning brightly, and all the presents seemed impossible to my despondent mind. I was sure that a confined existence in a mental hospital was in store for the rest of my life. I would live out the balance of my life exactly like Uncle Lee had. The opportunity to end my suffering would also be very unlikely (absolutely no chance of suicide).

After Christmas, a decision had been made as to what mental facility would be my next home. The same attending psychologist decided that due to my professional status in Syracuse, I should move somewhere out of town.

10

Strike Two

The doctor in charge of my care decided that the notoriety of my mental illness and attempted suicide would be less damaging to my professional reputation if I was transferred to a location far from Syracuse. Although there were several possibilities, his first choice was the McClean Institute outside of Boston. He had contacted a doctor at this facility and arranged for my transfer from Crouse Irving Memorial Hospital in Syracuse. Although I was still acutely suicidal, all medication was stopped so the new hospital in Massachusetts could start from scratch in my treatment. This would prove to be a huge mistake.

I wanted to go by car with Ruth but the doctor declined my request, deciding that a commercial flight from Syracuse to Logan Airport in Boston would be the best method. The thought of using up all my life savings on my care already was weighing on my messed-up mind. I doubted that my insurance would cover the airline tickets.

My expectations of exposure to the public when I left the hospital for the airport troubled me. I was sure that vast crowds of people would be there to witness this wacko veterinarian being flown to Boston to be incarcerated in a mental hospital. Besides Ruth and myself we also had to buy airline tickets for another gal who was supposed to secure my safety during the trip. I think she was a nurse who definitely was not qualified for the task at hand.

This gal certainly didn't have a clue about safety for a suicidal patient. She was very pleasant, about one hundred and twenty pounds, and obviously thought this was a great way to make eleven dollars an hour and get a free plane ride from Syracuse to Boston and back. It would not prove to be a pleasant trip for her.

I had no sedation and no restraint of any kind for the trip. The doctor had required that I stay in a wheelchair for the trip. Nothing secured me in the chair. Ruth had been told not to allow me to go in the men's room.

The exposure in Hancock Airport in Syracuse was horrifying. I almost always saw someone I knew whenever I went to the airport, but luckily I saw no one. I was very suicidal, wanted to die in the worst way, and wished that my previous attempt to die had been successful. The thought that this was a one-way ticket away from a wonderful home, exhausting my life savings for care in a mental hospital consumed my thinking. Fortunately, when the three of us finally got on the plane, no one seemed to recognize me.

The plan at Logan Airport upon our arrival was that personnel from the mental hospital were to be waiting for me upon arrival. When we disembarked at Logan, they were nowhere to be seen. We waited and waited and waited. My mind was filled with the hope that they would never arrive and that somehow I could find another method to end my suffering.

Eventually a group of three or four men in uniform approached our location with a stretcher on wheels. As they came closer, the heavy leather restraint straps on the stretcher were clearly visible. It was obvious that I was going to be strapped down on the stretcher like a wild animal for the trip to the mental hospital. These individuals definitely knew how to handle suicidal patients.

Somehow I just knew this would be a one-way ticket to a lifetime of incarceration in a mental hospital. When they were about twenty feet away from my wheelchair, I bolted out of the chair, ran as fast as I could, and leaped over a railing about fifty feet from where we were located. As I vaulted over the railing, I felt the hands of the one hundred and twenty pound nurse trying in vain to stop me. I had no idea what was over the railing, but I would soon find out.

It proved to be a forty foot fall onto a cement walkway below. My body splattered directly on the cement walkway below. Fortunately, I did not hit any pedestrians. Once again, my desperate wish for death was denied. I was badly injured but still alive.

Obviously the planned transfer to the mental hospital was impossible. They were not equipped to handle my severe injuries. Soon an ambulance was summoned and I was placed on a stretcher and rushed to Mass General Hospital's Emergency Room.

Examinations and x-rays revealed a long list of injuries. The biggest worry was a fracture of the first cervical vertebrate. If the patient survives, this almost always leaves the person a life-long quadriplegic. Miraculously, in my case, the spinal cord had not been severed. The next most serious injury was a burst fracture of the L-5 vertebrate in my lower back. This fracture caused spinal cord damage that would result in constant pain, plus major debilitation the rest of my life. My left elbow was fractured and there were multiple major bruises of soft tissue, but these were minor problems compared to the spinal fractures.

The fracture to my cervical vertebrate left my spinal cord unprotected and subject to further damage. A sudden movement of my head in a fall could possibly leave me a life-long quadriplegic. To prevent this possibility, the orthopedic doctors applied a halo splint. This apparatus encircles the head with four screws holding the skull from any movement at all. This halo splint is connected to a body cast around the chest by large steel rods. I would have to live with the halo for the next three months. The head remained absolutely fixed in the proper position allowing the vertebrate to heal.

The L-5 fracture was stabilized with two Harrington rods and the elbow fracture stabilized with a figure-eight application of stainless steel wire. I had used both of these procedures at my veterinary hospital in the past on injured dogs that were hit by cars.

Eventually I was transferred to a private room on the orthopedic floor. Although I was almost completely incapacitated by my injuries, my suicidal history mandated constant restraint to the bed with heavy leather straps. Besides the restraint, a nurse was assigned to watch over me at all hours of the day and night. One nurse was particularly compassionate. She had suffered from depression herself at one time in her life and confessed of her own suicidal thoughts at that time. She was very interested in my life and we chatted on and on for hours. Other nurses were less considerate, would not talk to me at all, and would treat me like a mad dog that was tied down.

One problem became obvious very soon after the admission to Mass General. I couldn't urinate. The fracture of the L-5 had destroyed the nerves innervating the bladder. Unfortunately, this was not a temporary problem, but the good news—I was not incontinent. This required catheterization four times a day and would be a requirement for the rest of my life. If I live to an age of ninety years, I will have catheterized myself over fifty-five thousand times. The L-5 injury also came very close to making me a paraplegic with paralysis to both legs. The nerves to the calf muscles in my lower legs were destroyed but the other leg muscles were still functional. The loss of the lower leg muscles removed all of the spring in my gait and I would walk like a duck for the rest of my life. Walking like a duck, however, is much better than not being able to walk at all—which was almost my fate.

Many of my friends and relatives still hadn't given up on me. Ruth was at my side all the time, but had to go back and forth to Fayetteville to keep tabs on the children. My sister Zoe, along with her sister-in-law, Katherine Goodwin, lived in nearby Haverhill, Massachusetts, were frequent visitors, as were Bob and Sally Watts from nearby Wayland. Brother Tom and sister Ada May flew out from home and a classmate from vet school, Dr. Alan Ahearne, flew up from Garden City, NY. I will be forever grateful to these special souls who still supported me, even after my second attempt to end my life. Any student of this illness will discover that repeated attempts at suicide are common in patients that don't recover.

When my injuries were stabilized, a decision had to be made as to where I would go next. It was decided that the psych ward at Strong Memorial Hospital in Rochester, NY would be my next stop. This would be closer to home for Ruth, especially since no one knew how long I would be there.

The method of transfer to Strong Memorial was quite different from my trip from Syracuse to Boston. Fortunately, it was determined that my insurance would pay for a private medical transfer (by air), which cost several thousand dollars. Even though my injuries still prevented me from walking, I was strapped to a stretcher with heavy leather straps on both arms and both feet. In addition to this restraint, a muscular attendant, who reminded me of Dick Butkus, was at my side at all times. The plane was very small with hardly enough room for the pilot, Ruth, "Dick Butkus," and me.

When we reached the Albany, NY area, the plane encountered a fierce winter storm with severe headwinds. This was the roughest plane ride I have ever experienced. Even the pilot was worried. Finally we reached Rochester, arriving over an hour later than scheduled due to the storm. Ruth remembers that the pilot breathed a big sigh of relief when the plane finally came to a stop.

Strong Memorial would be my home for the next two months. The first night was spent in a room with absolutely nothing in it except a bed—not even a window. A very muscular nurse sat by my bed the entire night. Obviously they were well aware of the proper way to care for suicidal patients. The new antidepressant medication started in Boston was helping. I was still very depressed but the acute suicidal urges had subsided. The second day I was transferred to a private room in the psych ward. All the windows were screened with steel grates, double locks on all doors, and absolutely nothing was glass or breakable: absolutely no possible opportunity to hurt yourself in any manner. The staff was excellent and treated all the patients with respect. Everyone was expected to be self-sufficient. In my own case, I had to use the bathroom, wash up, etc., with a walker and the halo splint. Every movement was extremely painful, but I did learn to care for myself. Progress and healing, however, were slow.

The time at Strong proved to be a study of mental illness. Everyone had a problem. The bipolar patients in the manic phase would be higher than a kite, but almost everyone else was obviously depressed. Electro-shock therapy, which is controversial, was used on several depressed patients. In my own case, this was not an option due to the presence of the halo splint. One young girl showed an amazing response to just one treatment. She was obviously from a wealthy family since she had a private nurse at her side constantly. She was so despondent that she would drag along behind the nurse showing no response to anyone or anything. The next day, after one electro-shock treatment, she was playing the piano, leading everyone in one song after another. I'd love to know if her recovery was permanent. She was obviously very talented with a very likeable personality.

The saddest part of mental illness is the effect it has on the friends and family of the patients. Our four children were still quite young, and I'm sure they struggled as a result of my illness, the suicide attempts, and the hospitalization in a lock-up. Ruth was terrific about bringing them in to see their father. The future prospect of our family happiness had to be horrifying to everyone. The hospital scheduled several family sessions where professionals would answer all the questions and try to keep families dealing with this terrible disease together.

During all of the time I spent in mental hospitals, I never met or even heard of anyone that made a complete recovery. Since almost all forms of mental illness are characterized by lengthy periods of illness, most patients lose hope for recovery. In recollecting these painful personal memories of my illness, I hope my story will help the patients and their families stay the course until complete recovery arrives (sometimes taking years).

Eventually we were informed that my insurance would no longer pay for any further hospitalization in a mental hospital. The professionals at Strong indicated that I was still seriously depressed. They based their decision on the results of a blood test measuring a certain function of the pituitary gland, which apparently was consistent with depression. (What they didn't know, that would show up later, was that I had a pituitary tumor the size of a golf ball.) The doctors wanted me to pay personally for the extended hospital stay until they felt my depression had lifted. This I refused to do.

Just before my release, the halo splint was removed and I went home (something I thought would never happen). Before I could be released, I had to agree to see a psychiatrist in Syracuse twice a week and stay on a lot of medication. It was March 7, 1986. Depression would continue to plague my energy and happiness for the next fourteen years, but I would never attempt to end my life again.

11

The Hard Road Back

Believe me, it is very difficult to regain self-respect, confidence, and the respect of others when you return from hospitalization due to mental illness. My reputation was pretty much destroyed. Fortunately, Dr. Ed Chapman, who had joined the practice in 1977, was very popular with the clients, and the practice had survived my extended absence very well. Other veterinarians that helped out during my absence were Dr. David Taylor, Dr. Jerald Shing, and Dr. Harold Jenkins. I felt drugged most of the time due to all the medication I was on and had a constant tremor. All of the above made the return to a routine of a busy profession very difficult. Caring for me at home was much easier on Ruth, but the future was still a big worry for all of us. The biggest lift I found was being able to get back to my farm and the horses.

In an attempt to add a little joy to our lives, Ruth and I spent a week in Bermuda the last week of April of 1986. This was our first trip to Bermuda since our honeymoon and proved to be good medicine for both of us. I was still crippled but did manage to ride the motorbikes and tour this delightful island.

Returning home, my confidence in facing friends and clients improved somewhat and I began to take some office calls and do some surgery. Many old faithful clients requested to see me, which I was delighted to do. I specifically remember Wendy and Phil Jefferis, who still thought I was the greatest. They even named their two dogs after me. One they named *Jim* and the other they named *Marshall*.

On June 21, 1986, I was able to escort Cynthia down the aisle to join her great husband, Sam Vulcano, in marriage. I was still in terrible shape, but Cynthia vowed that she would not walk down the aisle unless I was the escort. My full recovery was still a big question mark for everyone, especially myself. My recollection of the summer of 1986 was that of just trying to hang in. I continued to visit the psychiatrist, take my medicine, and try to survive. Feeling good was not the case, but being able to be home with no grates on the windows or double locks on the doors was definitely progress.

I often reflect that if I just knew someone who had survived suicide and hospitalization, it would have helped a lot at that point in my life. On most days full recovery seemed impossible, but I continued to hang in. The reply of our minister to my question if he knew anyone who had survived suicide and made it back was forever etched in my memory—"Why, no, I don't know anyone who has."

12

The Brain Tumor

On November 7, 1986, I had an appointment with Dr. John Lubicky, an orthopedic surgeon and great guy who was following the progress of all my fractures. During the appointment, I asked John if he could arrange a brain scan for me. I explained that my older brother, Fred, had had a brain tumor, and even though I had been hospitalized for a long time in three different hospitals, a brain scan was never done. I just wanted this done for peace of mind. He made a call and I was able to have one done the same day.

The next morning I went to the farm early and returned home at about eleven to get ready to leave for the Syracuse-Navy football game at the Carrier Dome where we had season tickets. For some reason that I couldn't understand, Ruth was acting very strange. This continued all afternoon.

Finally, when we returned home, she said, "You have to sit down. I have something to tell you." She explained that Dr. Lubicky had called earlier that morning, very nervous, with the news, "You'll have to tell Jim he has a brain tumor the size of a golf ball on his pituitary gland."

My initial reaction was total shock and disbelief. After a few minutes, I started to feel a strong sense of relief—at last a possible explanation for my downward spiral of nine years starting in 1977, a possible reason why I never improved. This emotion was followed by one of anger. Why couldn't someone have ordered a scan much earlier??? Why did I have to spend all that money and take twenty-five different drugs when I had a brain tumor all along??? Why did I have to request a scan myself after seeing all those doctors and being hospitalized in three different hospitals over a period of two years???

Finally I settled down and we started to think about what would be our next step. Since I had an appointment that Monday with the psychiatrist, we decided to wait and discuss this finding with him first. He was very defensive (why hadn't he asked for a scan himself), explaining that the tumor was incidental and had nothing to do with my long-standing depression.

81

I just couldn't buy this opinion and decided to talk with our good friend, Dr. Bill Stewart, a neurosurgeon who had operated on my brother Fred. Bill explained that any growth that size was very likely to cause a problem. He strongly recommended surgical removal and his first choice was Dr. Edward Laws at the Mayo Clinic in Rochester, Minnesota. Dr. Laws had previously operated on a colleague of mine, Dr. John Cummings, an anatomy professor at Cornell and I immediately called John as a reference. John's experience with Dr. Laws was excellent so this readily became our first choice as well.

Bill Stewart arranged an appointment with Dr. Laws on January 27, 1987.

The Mayo Clinic in the relatively small town of Rochester, Minnesota, is just an amazing facility rising majestically from the level plains of the Midwest. You can get a complete medical work-up in one day without ever leaving the building (from head to toe).

Our appointment with Dr. Laws went very well. He explained the risks with the surgery, one of which was death, but Ruth and I immediately knew I had found the best possible surgeon for this type of surgery in the world. Dr. Laws uses a "transphenoidal" approach to remove the pituitary tumors, which are located at the base of the brain. The surgery is completed using fiber optic instruments. First an incision is made above the upper incisor teeth; the nose is basically moved to one side, opening the skull from the sinus cavity behind the nose. The tumor is then removed using fiber optic instruments. At that time, Dr. Laws had a daughter studying veterinary medicine at Tufts University near Boston. We immediately bonded and instantly became good friends.

While checking out my depressive illness at Mayo, I was fortunate to meet Dr. Lin, my very favorite psychiatrist of all time. We also became good friends and have stayed in touch with each other for many years. Our last connection was at the Mayo Clinic in Jacksonville, Florida, where he enjoys the winters better than in Minnesota.

On January 30, 1987, Dr. Laws removed my golf ball sized tumor without incident. Our daughter, Cynthia, who had recently married, surprised us by flying out to Minnesota to keep her mother company while waiting for the outcome of the surgery. To prevent the possibility of brain swelling following the surgery, large doses of steroids are administered before and after the surgery. The mental effect of the steroids is an unbelievable euphoria. I enjoyed a tremendous high for several days following the surgery; just like someone who wins the lottery.

The stay at the hospital lasted five days. In the phone book at Mayo the following script appeared: "Adversity causes some men to break—others to break records." I prayed that I could join those that go on to break records. On our way back to the hotel, we passed a photography shop. I was so euphoric; I went in and asked the owner if he would take a picture of Ruth and I (five days post-op from brain surgery). He took our picture, which I treasure to this day. Removal of the tumor definitely helped my depressive illness, but it was not a complete cure. It would be another thirteen years before I would truly feel completely cured.

Before leaving Mayo, I visited the special clinic there in St. Mary's Hospital that dealt exclusively with patients' bladder problems. Since I was unable to urinate, they suggested that I try a two-week program to possibly correct this problem. I decided to give it a try and scheduled a time in April to return when they had an opening.

On Saturday, February 7, 1987, Ruth and I returned home. Our whole family met us at the airport. We proceeded to Riley's Restaurant for a wonderful dinner in a private room.

The kids had decorated the house with balloons and welcome home banners. Returning home that day was one of the greatest joys of my life. I had lived through the darkest days life has to offer and survived. To return to my wonderful home and recognize the love my family still had for me was the greatest reward I had ever received.

The next Sunday morning, I decided to attend our church service. Ruth was tied up with a million things to do after being away, so I went by myself. Previously, I had joined a special group of church members who had made major contributions to help pay for the renovation of the sanctuary. I was still feeling good and thought the members would welcome me back following the brain surgery. This, however, was definitely not the case. I was shunned and ignored completely that morning. Sympathy for mental health victims has improved greatly in recent years, but at that time, anyone who tried to end his own life was considered a pariah and was not a welcomed part of the congregation.

When I returned home, I announced to Ruth that I would meet the Lord at my farm in the future on Sunday mornings. I never returned to services at the church again, and no one from church ever called to see how I was doing.

I would like to assure all parents, relatives, or friends of suicide victims that God has welcomed them into heaven just the same as if they died from a heart attack or other health problem. The teaching that suicide is an unforgivable sin by some organized religions, in my opinion, is just not true. The good Lord has blessed my life beyond belief since my two suicide attempts.

This does not apply to murder-suicide victims. I believe there is no place in heaven for those that take another life or commit a terrible crime and then take their own life to avoid prosecution. War conditions and arts of self defense are legitimate exceptions. During my years of depression, I often wanted to end my own life, but never, never had any thought of harming anyone else.

13

Mayo Revisited

On April 20, 1987, I returned to St. Mary's Hospital at the Mayo Clinic for the two-week program to improve the bladder function. I was on a floor together with many other patients who had paralysis problems due to different causes—strokes, automobile accidents, cancer surgery, etc. St. Mary's is a huge facility with a thousand-bed capacity. It is probably the only large hospital in the world where a patient can walk down the road a short distance to a golf driving range and hit golf balls into a cornfield. I had complete freedom and did this on a few occasions.

A couple times a week the staff would take all the patients on a special bus to nearby Silver Lake Park for a couple hours of rest and relaxation. Since I could walk, I joined the nurses in helping get the patients on and off the bus. It was a gorgeous facility with numerous paved pathways winding around beautiful lakes. I especially recall wheeling an elderly lady who had both legs removed. She had grown up on a farm in the west and we chatted all afternoon about our common farm heritage. The park was on the Mississippi flyway for Canadian geese. That afternoon we were surrounded by thousands of these beautiful birds.

This experience sparked an idea that I would use later in my foundation at the farm. Helping this lady that afternoon resulted in a lift in my depression while helping someone worse off than myself. I immediately knew this would work in depression therapy and the theme for my foundation was born: *When you help someone—you help yourself.*

During my stay at St. Mary's, I got acquainted with two special patients. One was Misty, a beautiful young gal who had been in a bad car accident resulting in brain damage and paralysis. The other was Jamie, a gorgeous twelve-year-old girl with paralysis due to a birth defect. A lot of my free time was spent trying to cheer them up.

The return trip to Mayo was a total failure as far as improving my bladder function. Apparently the nerve damage was too extensive and no return of normal function was possible. The personal experience interacting with patients worse off than I definitely improved my depression. Although the complete cure of my depressive illness was still thirteen years away, I did find out that interaction and assisting others was definitely therapeutic. Before I left Mayo I informed Misty and Jamie that if the two foals due to be born a month later were fillys, I would name them *Misty* and *Jamie*. As it turned out, both foals were colts, but I named them *JMF's Misty* and *JMF's Jamie* after the girls anyway. Both of these horses proved to be winners.

The girls were thrilled to have those horses named after them and we have stayed in touch with each other for years. Jamie's progress has been fantastic. Misty continues to struggle with her adversity.

When I returned home I soon realized that my life as a busy practitioner of Veterinary Medicine would never be the same. News of my mental illness and incarceration in a mental hospital spread rapidly in the small village of Fayetteville and adjacent areas. Some clients went elsewhere, but because of Dr. Chapman and the excellent staff, our practice was still very healthy.

My previous excellent reputation had taken a big hit and I could see the hand writing on the wall. One client asked if I was still competent to do surgery on her dog.

Thank God I had the farm. The horses welcomed me back with their unconditional love. The birth of the first two foals to be born on the farm was exciting. (*JMF's Misty* and *JMF's Jamie*.) Witnessing the miracle of creation in the birth of these wobbly-legged babies is terrific therapy for depression. This revelation and other tangible benefits led me to adapt the slogan: *where animals help people.*

The farm was my passion and therapy for my illness. It brought me back to my roots and rekindled the happy days of growing up on our family farm. Although I was rather limited in energy and ambition, I did manage after thirteen years to build the two entrance roads, the JMF stone pillars at the entrance, eleven horse shelters, twenty-one paddocks and pastures, a quarter-mile of water lines, half a mile of drainage pipe, a six stall addition to the main stable, a twenty car parking lot, and an indoor heated swimming pool for horses that we use year round.

Operating the backhoe, the bulldozer, the two tractors, and dump wagon was great therapy and prevented a relapse of major depression like the one I survived in the fall of 1985.

June 12, 1987, marked my thirtieth reunion from Cornell Vet College. Everyone knew about my illness and it was obvious that they didn't know what to expect or what to say when Ruth and I arrived. I was far from being fully recovered, but returning to friends and colleagues was helpful and necessary for my healing process. It was obvious that everyone was rooting for me to return to the happy-go-lucky Jim Marshall they knew in Vet school. Fifteen years later, in 2002 at our forty-fifth reunion, I think I showed them that I had fully recovered. Hopefully, I can convince them to support my foundation financially in future years. All of my classmates have been successful practicing in our great profession.

July 30, 1987, was the six-month anniversary of my brain surgery at the Mayo clinic. I celebrated the occasion by purchasing *The Vet's Pet* in Maine. *The Vet's Pet* is a nineteen-foot outboard motor boat that we enjoy every summer on the coast of Maine. Most boat owners will describe a boat as: "A hole in the water where you place lots of money." That has proven to be the case with *The Vet's Pet*. Salt water takes its toll on outboard motors and repairs are constant and expensive. I purchased a new Yamaha four stroke 115 horsepower engine for the *Pet* in 2002 when the original motor (rebuilt many times) finally gave up for good and quit! The cost for the new motor; an unbelievable ten grand. The ability to have your own boat to tour the absolutely beautiful coast of Maine in July, August, and September is a luxury I hope I never have to give up.

On March 6, 1988, our daughter, Cynthia, gave birth to our first grandchild—Samuel James Vulcano, who we now call *Broadway Slam*. At the time of this writing we have seven additional grandchildren and they are the loves of our lives! *Slam* is now fifteen and loves the farm and can operate just about all the equipment very well. The greatest phone call that I have ever received at six-thirty in the morning: "Grampy can you pick me up and take me to the farm today?" Then of course we have to go to the Hamlet Diner in Chittenango where *Slam* downs a breakfast fit for a lumberjack. I sincerely hope all of my grandkids will want to go to the farm with Grampy.

In June of 1988, I started to think about possible litigation malpractice regarding the negligence in my previous medical care. I reviewed the failure to diagnose the brain tumor and the negligence involved in the second suicide attempt at Logan Airport with two prominent attorneys in Syracuse, who specialized in Medical Malpractice. After reviewing the facts, they concluded that I had an excellent chance to recover several million dollars in damages. After weighing this decision for some time I cancelled the lawsuit! I felt I just couldn't enjoy spending money that I hadn't earned myself. There is no question that mistakes were made that caused me much pain and suffering. However, I felt better about getting back on my feet and supporting my family with my own efforts. The one doctor in particular was very lucky to get off the hook. The attorneys were very upset with me. They felt we had a very strong case, a great possibility for a large settlement, and a large contingency fee for themselves.

14

That Constant Burning Pain

The burst fracture of my fifth lumbar vertebra in Boston left me with a constant (sometimes unbearable) burning pain in my lower back. Painkilling medication had absolutely no beneficial effect. I also tried a *TENS* unit, which you strap to your back. This sends electrical impulses into the area and is supposed to alter the message of pain received by the brain. The *TENS* was also no help.

At an office call with Dr. Lubicky in June of 1989, he suggested that I check out the Spine Clinic in Minneapolis, Minnesota, which is world renowned—specializing only with problems in our spines. On June 19, 1989, Ruth and I flew out for an appointment at the Spine Clinic. After reviewing the films of an MRI study of my fractured vertebra, the doctor informed us that surgery (anterior decompression of the fifth lumbar vertebra) would have a 98 percent chance of eliminating all the pain in my lower spine.

The decision to go for it was a no-brainer, so Ruth and I once again flew out to Minnesota for the surgery on September 29, 1989. This was a major operation. An incision was made from the center of my stomach all the way around to the spine in the back. (I still have the scar to prove it.) The surgeon then removed the front portion of the fifth lumbar vertebra relieving pressure on the spinal cord. The doctor indicated that when I woke up from this very lengthy operation the constant burning pain would be gone. Ruth and I were anxious to see how I felt upon waking up from the general anesthesia. However, as soon as I came to, the same constant burning pain prevailed: no change what-so-ever! The surgery was a total failure—actually leaving me worse off. Following the surgery, I received too much Demerol (a pain killer) causing my normal intestinal activity (peristalsis) to stop completely. This caused excessive gas to accumulate in the intestines and I bloated like a dead frog. The bloating caused the surgical incision to weaken resulting in a surgical hernia that would require further surgery. The no-brainer decision to operate was not a good one!

The only good thing to happen to me on this trip to the Spine Clinic in Minneapolis was a visit from our good friends from Detroit Lakes, Minnesota. Ruth and I had met three wonderful couples on Sanibel Island, Florida, several years earlier. I became the fourth in their golfing group and we became good friends—getting together on Sanibel on several winter vacations. Dave Knutson, a radio station executive and his wife, Henri, organized our activities. Dr. Bob Watson, a retired physician, and his wife Dolores made sure we all stayed in good health. Bob Irvine, a colorful, charismatic attorney and his wife, Eloise, kept us all out of jail. These good friends made the long drive down from Detroit Lakes and surprised me at the hospital. I was very despondent after the surgery failure and their visit was very therapeutic. They all will be very treasured friends for life.

Shortly after returning home I had to fly to New York City for a meeting. On the flight down I sat next to a friendly gal who liked to chat. The conversation eventually led to me recounting my recent trip to the Spine Clinic for surgery. She also had problems with back pain and told me about a surgeon in New York City who had operated on her back also, with limited success. She went on to describe the special surgical approach this doctor used to relieve painful conditions of the spine. She had his phone number and I jotted it down. One thing she said about this doctor: "He isn't cheap—you have to pay five thousand dollars up front before the surgery."

One thing certain about people in constant pain: They will go anywhere and pay anything for a chance of relief. I was no exception.

Since I had a few hours before my return flight, I decided to call the doctor who had a cancellation and told me to come right over.

Waiting in the office, I started talking with another couple from Long Island. The man next to me told me all about his wife's pain and previous surgery. She was waiting for a post-surgical check-up and her pain was obvious. She kept moving, trying to find a position that would relieve her pain. He went on to add: "This doctor isn't cheap—you have to pay ten thousand dollars up front before the surgery." Obviously his fees were going up.

Following his examination of my back, the doctor thought that there was an excellent possibility that his special surgical procedure would completely relieve my constant pain. I agreed to mail him copies of previous MRI films for him to evaluate.

Shortly before Christmas, this doctor's receptionist called to tell me that the films confirmed his optimism. He wanted me to show up at the hospital on December twenty-seventh at seven in the morning ready for surgery. She also added: "Make sure that you bring two checks: One for one-hundred dollars for the cardiologist to check me before surgery and another for fifteen thousand dollars for the surgeon." I made out the check for one-hundred dollars, but left the other one blank—I wanted to talk with the doctor. An inquiry with my insurance indicated that twelve thousand five hundred dollars was the upper limit. When I confronted the doctor he responded: "I'll give you a deal and accept the twelve-five."

The surgery time turned out to be forty-five minutes total. Once again, when the anesthesia wore off, the constant burning pain was unaltered and the surgeon was off to Jamaica for a vacation, financed by my twelve-five. After hearing these stories, it is easy to understand one reason for rising insurance premiums.

I still had the surgical hernia from Minneapolis to correct. On February 25, 1990, the hernia was surgically corrected at the George Washington Hospital in D.C. Dr. Edward Laws, the trusted surgeon who removed my brain tumor had transferred to Head of Surgery at GWU and arranged a soft tissue surgeon to do the surgery. The results were excellent and we also got to visit our daughter Jennifer who was a student at GWU.

While at the GWU hospital, I talked with a neurologist who felt that my pain was due to Ischemia (loss of blood supply) to an area deep in the spinal cord at L5 from the accident. The surgery I had in Minneapolis and NYC actually had no chance of relieving my pain. The only thing that improved from the surgery was the bank accounts of the surgeons involved.

Over the next few years I still clung to the very remote possibility that my body was rejecting the presence of all the surgical hardware in my back. My hope was that the Harrington rods, steel wires, and clips still remaining in my back could be involved. Finally, on November 9, 1994, a surgeon friend of mine in Boston removed every bit of hardware from my back. In my years of practice, I had seen rare cases when animals would reject steel plates, rods, screws, etc. which had to be removed.

The surgeon, a friend, removed them at no cost to me as a favor. The surgery helped my peace of mind that I had tried everything, but the pain remained the same. Presently (2004) I have endured the constant burning pain now for eighteen years. When I am extremely active on the farm, I can block it out. However, I do feel that if I ever become confined to bed rest or a nursing home, the pain will become hell to live with.

Presently, some success is being achieved by the implantation of a spinal cord stimulator, which is surgically implanted on the spinal cord at the injured site. This is connected to a battery-powered source that is placed under the skin, similar to a cardiac Pace Maker. Presently I have decided to live with the pain rather than go for more surgery and possibly more disappointment.

The prediction by our medical people is that in the near future: "No one will have to live with pain." I hope they are right, because an awful lot of people besides me live each day with pain.

15

My Equine Therapists

During the years of depression the greatest therapists that kept me clinging to life and the hope of recovery were the many different horses that resided at the farm at one time or another.

The absolute magnificence of the horse has captured the love and admiration of both men and women since time began.

I'm not going to tell you all of them, but I do have to tell you about a few that were extra special to me. All horses that are born on the farm have the JMF prefix and are always named after a person I admire. Unfortunately the only attribute that counts in race-horses is speed. Beauty, personality, temperament, and size are great, but speed is the quality that pays the bills. As parents we all want our kids to play basketball just like Michael Jordan, but that's a dream that rarely comes true. Our kids can succeed by using their many other talents, yet that is not true with race-horses. Speed and the time it takes to run a mile is the only path to achieve fame and success.

I have written an addendum to this chapter in the appendix, listing all the details of my favorite horses. If you are a real racehorse fan, you might find that section interesting.

I have to tell you about two special horses that pull carriages at our *Walk & Talk* sessions at the farm. One is a retired racehorse and one is a draft horse.

The retired harness horse is a beautiful black Standardbred named *Jiggs Fraizer*. *Jiggs* is owned by the Morrisville College Foundation and leased to our Foundation. He is a very famous trotter who holds trotting records at five different County Fair tracks across New York State. The students at Morrisville College enjoyed driving *Jiggs* in the many fair races. He would almost always win!

At the farm, *Jiggs* pulls a beautiful four-wheeled Surrey that I had custom built by an Amish carriage maker in Intercourse, Pennsylvania. A ride around the track with *Jiggs* is a definite favorite form of therapy for our depressed visitors.

Jiggs also pulls a special handicapped accessible cart on occasion. This is a special cart that I welded together that accommodates a wheelchair. The back of the cart folds down forming a ramp. The patient in the wheelchair can be pushed up on the cart right behind *Jiggs*. There is room for another seat right beside the wheelchair. *Jiggs* will trot around the track almost by himself. Once he is underway, I like to hand the reins over to the handicapped passenger. They are absolutely thrilled to be driving a horse for the first time in their lives.

Often people with severe physical handicaps also battle depression, but not always. Although they have so many reasons to be depressed, I have seen several paraplegics and quadriplegics that have a marvelous positive and happy outlook on life. Christopher Reeve is obviously one of these special individuals.

The other regular pulling a carriage at our *Walk & Talk* sessions is *Big Bad Ben the Blonde Belgian*. *Ben* is a huge draft horse weighing almost a ton. He is as gentle as he is big, and a clear favorite of the visitors.

When I purchased the new wedding carriage made in Canada, I realized the Standardbreds were not strong enough to pull this carriage that can accommodate up to nine adults.

My search ended when I found *Ben*. He was one half of a Belgian team that was used in pulling contests. *Ben* was not a good puller. He was too much of a pussy cat to be a good puller. I had to pay two thousand dollars to buy him, but he has proven to be worth every penny.

Ben and the wedding carriage were waiting outside the church in North Chittenango this summer to escort the minister's daughter and her husband from the church to the limo.

He was also an entry in the *2003 Oz Parade* in downtown Chittenango. The appearance of *Big Bad Ben the Blonde Belgian* was definitely a crowd pleaser. The entry won the *Lion Award*, for best large animal presentation.

Ben and *Jiggs* will be available at the farm, together with the other animals to volunteer their services for therapy. They do not charge a fee. The equine therapy has definitely helped my depression, and I am sure it will help others as well.

My oldest grandson Sam Vulcano joins me and Ben in the 2003 Oz Parade

16

The 1990s

The decade of the 90s would prove to be ten more years of depressive illness—some years worse than others. The stock market went up, but I went down. Presently, March 1, 2004, I am confident that the 90s were hard to survive, but they finally did bring an end to my illness. At the very end of the decade I would find a cure.

On April 1, 1990, I sold my Veterinary Hospital and practice to Ed Chapman. Ed had been a terrific associate since 1977 and was anxious to own his own hospital. Over these thirteen years he had adopted my style of handling patients and clients.

Over several years every practice develops a certain type of clientele. Some cater to the very wealthy, see selectively few patients, and charge extremely high fees for their services. Believe it or not, there are people who enjoy being fleeced and boast at parties about spending two thousand dollars on their *Fifi*.

I always tried to make our services affordable and excellent. We never catered to clients that couldn't wait their turn on busy days. As a result, we had lots of happy clients. We would see thirty to fifty office calls a day in addition to the farm calls. Ed has continued this tradition.

Sometimes when a practice is sold to a professional with a very different philosophy the client numbers decline rapidly.

I knew that Ed would be successful and the clients happy with him. Although I had no plans to retire, depression had eroded my interest in the practice. If I didn't sell, Ed would have likely opened a practice in the area and taken several clients with him.

For many years, serving on the NYS Board of Examiners of Veterinary Medicine, I had seen several practitioners that just practiced too long. They didn't update their hospitals, keep proper records, and would be stripped of their state license to practice by dissatisfied clients that reported them to the OPD, which is the Office of Professional Discipline. OPD investigates the charges and the professional license to practice is often revoked. This is a very sad way to end a long professional career.

Although it was a very painful decision, I sold the practice and hospital that was started twenty-eight years previously. It is now thirteen years later and I have no regrets. Ed has kept most of the old clients and added new ones. He has maintained the building in excellent condition. I stop in several days each week since we live right behind the hospital. The entire staff always welcomes my visits and makes me feel like a Professor Emeritus.

Many times during the sale of a practice, hard feelings develop over financial or other issues between the professionals. This results in bad blood and the original Vet never returns to his old practice. Fortunately, our transfer went smoothly. We are the best of friends and Ed is one of the major contributors to my Foundation.

On June 13, 1990, I received my P-license to drive horses in paramutual races. I was fifty-seven years old and I never thought the officials would grant me a license. I guess they thought I was qualified, but my driving career was short-lived. Although some older drivers participate, driving is definitely better suited to youth. I did win one paramutual race driving *JMF's Misty*. This was a terrific thrill, but I soon realized that it was no place for my old bones. My wife was also very much in favor of my retirement. There is always a chance of going down in a race and getting trampled on by all of the horses behind you. I had some close calls driving at county fairs, but luckily I was never hurt. I decided to quit driving before my luck ran out. I still train at the farm several times a week, but this is relatively safe.

In June of 1992, my son Peter started a twelve-week Farrier course at the Cornell Veterinary College. Keeping shoes on race-horses is expensive. Since the feet are constantly growing, the shoes have to be removed, the hooves trimmed, and new shoes tacked back on. The average cost is fifty to seventy dollars per horse every three to four weeks. Following the course at Cornell, Peter does all the Farrier work on our horses. This allows us to eliminate much of the cost of maintaining our race-horses. I do the Vet work, Peter does the shoeing, and we both share the training. Peter takes care of all the work at the race track, allowing Ruth and I to sit up in the grandstand having dinner and watching the races.

Attending the races at nearby Vernon Downs is a wonderful spot to have dinner. On a beautiful summer evening the windows of the grandstand are open. The view of the horses, the colorful drivers, the seven-eighths mile racing oval, and the rolling hills in the distance is spectacular. Peter always brings our horses out to warm up between races and he wears the same helmet and white, brown, and gold colors that I had used. Once in a while we win a race and enjoy the trip down to the winners circle.

Vernon Downs and other tracks in New York State have had trouble surviving in recent years. In 2003, a law was passed in the state to legalize video slot machines at race tracks. This is expected to revitalize harness racing in the state.

The regulation of drug surveillance in race-horses is badly in need of change. The reputation of the sport has been tarnished by published reports of horses racing on illegal drugs. Many potential fans are turned off. They feel horses are drugged, and races are fixed. As a result, they have turned their affection to car races. It seems there are millions that love watching these cars go at astronomical speeds and often crash as a result. These accidents often result in the drivers getting seriously hurt, burned, or even killed. To me this spectacle seems sadistic. I prefer to watch the Equine athletes compete.

We have one great advantage over automobiles and that is the magnificence of the horse. Books and movies about horse heroes like *Seabiscuit* will definitely help return the popularity of horse racing.

Having observed the activities of trainers for nearly twenty years, I can tell you that almost every horse receives some kind of drug to help them reach their potential.

Over 90 percent of these drugs are humane. Their action is not harmful to the horse, does not interfere with pain or normal fatigue, and helps the horse maintain good health when stressed with the excessive exercise of racing.

Drugs are definitely here to stay for man and animals. There are very few people who do not take a vitamin pill or medication of some kind on a daily basis to maintain good health. Shouldn't the horses have the same opportunity?

The problem arises when drugs that are inhumane are given to horses. These are drugs that cover up normal pain allowing the horse to injure themselves as a result. This includes patent pain killers like cocaine, Novocain, Butazoliden, and other similar drugs. Milk Shaking or the administration of large doses of bicarbonate of soda is inhumane. This ties up lactic acid (a result of muscle fatigue) blocking the normal fatigue of the horse. Mind-altering drugs are also inhumane causing overexertion and injury as a result. This includes amphetamines, crack cocaine, ecstasy, and other street drugs.

Every horse, like every human, has a God-given athletic potential. If the trainers and owners allow them to compete at this level, most horses will hold up and compete for years.

The problem arises when we try to make them exceed their ability by injecting sore joints with cortisone (which can destroy the cartilage) or giving them other inhumane medications. These practices can cause permanent disability and the poor horses can end up in the slaughter house as a result.

With the technology available today, I believe this problem can be solved. However, I see no activity or interest in our horse organizations to change. They seem content to live with our present bad image with the fans.

One suggestion I have made is to do a simple CBC (complete blood count) two hours before post time on each horse and make the results available to the fans. The smart handicappers will soon know a healthy blood count from a bad one. Horses that are obviously sick would be scratched and not be forced to race if they are ill. There is equipment available today that can complete this test on a drop of blood quickly and economically. This addition would convince the fans that the racing organization and officials are changing to humane treatment of horses. The fans would return to horse races in droves.

Almost a year ago I sent these suggestions to the New York State Racing and Wagering Board and also to the executive director of the United States Trotting Association in Columbus, Ohio. Do you want to know the result? Absolutely nothing, not even an acknowledgment of my letter. I am hopeful that eventually these officials will open their eyes and endorse a major overhaul of drug surveillance in race-horses. Once these changes are made, horse racing has an opportunity to return to the popularity it once enjoyed.

One of the rare, fun activities I enjoyed in the early 90s was playing Santa at the farm each Christmas. Our grandchildren at that time still believed in Santa. I purchased a Santa suit and would arrive at the main stable driving *National Star*. Several friends with young children were invited, and they would watch *Santa* and *Star* circle the track and then carry the big bag of presents up the stairs to the lounge over the stable. One by one these precious youngsters would climb up on my lap and receive their gifts.

Depression resulted in every activity being a real effort. I wanted to lie in bed or on the couch, but I am glad I forced myself to play Santa for a few years. It was fun.

On August 23, 1993, my brother Fred passed away. This loss drove me deeper into the depths of despair. Fred was a terrific individual that never had a chance of reaching his potential in life. The benign brain tumor that ravaged his life probably started growing at a fairly young age.

Despite this undiagnosed condition, he succeeded in farming and was voted Madison County Young Farmer of the Year in 1965. As time went on we all knew that Fred was not well, but doctors reported that he was in the best of health.

One day he stopped at our house on the way to Syracuse and told me that once in a while his vision would black out for a few seconds. I immediately knew that he had a serious brain malfunction of some kind, so I called Bill Stewart, a friend of ours who was a neurosurgeon. Bill offered to see him right away but Fred thought that he should go through his local doctor in Munnsville with the referral.

The local doctor was very upset that he was listening to the opinion of a Veterinarian and told Fred that he just needed a new pair of glasses. Since Fred persisted in his request to see a neurosurgeon, he referred him to Dr. Naumon in Syracuse.

A quick exam with an opthamaloscope revealed the problem. The optic nerves were bulging into the vitreous humor of his eyes. He also discovered that Fred's sense of smell had almost disappeared. It was obvious that Fred had a brain tumor. Fred was immediately admitted into Crouse Irving Hospital and would not get back home for four months. When Dr. Naumon found out about our friendship with Bill Stewart he transferred Fred to Bill for the required surgery.

X-rays and biopsies would confirm that Fred had a huge Benign Meningioma the size of a small grapefruit. The tumor had obviously been developing undiagnosed for years. Surgery five years earlier would have been much simpler, but now the size presented a huge challenge to the surgeon.

Surgery took eleven hours from start to finish. Controlling hemorrhage was a big problem. A large section of the skull had to be removed and frozen. The plan was to replace the bone six to eight weeks later.

Following surgery, the body temperature had to be kept as low as possible to prevent brain swelling. To accomplish this, Fred had to lie on a special mattress of ice water for hours. I felt so sorry for him lying there shivering.

I can't remember how many times Fred went back for surgery, but I know that it was several. There was absolutely no end to the complications. Excessive fluid built up in his brain and this required a shunt, which is a long tube that went from the ventricles of the brain down to his jugular vein.

His original skull bone did not heal properly, requiring a special plastic prosthesis to finally cover the surgical site. Before the final prosthesis was in place, Fred looked like a Dick Tracy character with a huge indentation in his skull. Only skin covered his brain. He had to wear a protective helmet at all times.

All of this surgery took a toll on Fred's life and he never regained his health. He required a lot of care and it was difficult to put up with his foul moods. As is often the case in geriatric illness, he would lash out in anger at his wife and children who loved him the most.

Finally the family decided that a nursing home would be a better place for Fred to receive the required care. He was moved to the Stonehedge Nursing Home in Chittenango. This location was on the way to the farm for me and I would stop and visit him several times a week.

It bothered me to see him in this environment. He was such a bear to live with that I couldn't bring him to our home. Finally I thought I could care for him at the farm if I could build a bedroom adjacent to the lounge and kitchen that was already present over the main stable. After this was constructed, with the approval of the doctors and his family, we moved Fred to the farm.

For several months Fred was happy. He was a true farmer and enjoyed being back on the farm even though he was living in a horse barn. I would make his breakfast every morning and he improved with his ability to partially care for himself. Fred knew scores of people in Madison County and the stream of visitors was endless. Brian Carlson, an unemployed friend, also with problems, became a daily companion. Brian did have a driver's license and the two of them would tour the many small diners in Madison County where Fred knew almost everyone.

This arrangement worked so well that I decided to move a house trailer on the farm so that Fred could have his own living quarters. Farms could apply for permits for trailers only to house individuals working on the farm. I convinced the local building inspector that Fred would qualify. Fred and Brian began a trailer search. They found a trailer for sale in Pompey. A seemingly nice couple had a trailer they lived in while building a new house. Once the house was completed they had to get rid of the trailer.

I let Fred take care of the entire purchase, which he did. He paid way too much for the trailer, but he had the necessary funds. Fred was excited to be taking control of his life and his angry outbursts towards his younger brother Jim were disappearing.

Getting approval for the septic system for the trailer proved to be a real challenge. Finally I built a system that satisfied the local inspector. It did not meet Madison County specifications, but since the location was over five hundred feet from New Boston Road, these requirements were waived.

After installing a water line, electrical line, and telephone, Fred was ready to move into his new home.

Earlier Fred purchased a brand new golf cart that even had his name proudly across the front. He delighted driving his visitors around the farm in his own vehicle.

Life in his new home on the farm would prove to be short-lived. Soon after moving into the trailer, Fred started experiencing severe seizures. This required around-the-clock surveillance and caring for him at the farm became difficult.

The decision to return to the nursing home had to be made. It was a huge disappointment for me. Fred would remain in Stonehedge until his death, ten days after his sixty-third birthday. However, I was glad that he enjoyed almost a year living on the farm. Fred had a wonderful sense of humor and I miss him greatly. Life is not fair to many people and this certainly was the case with beloved brother Fred.

At the time of his burial in the Stockbridge cemetery, the undertaker really screwed up. As the pall bearers moved Fred's casket over the dug grave, one side of the staging collapsed and the casket almost fell into the grave head first. I can still hear Fred laughing as hard as he could from inside the casket that this was the final screw up in his screwed-up life.

Following Fred's death I divided the cost of Fred's trailer and golf cart equally five ways. This was distributed to his widow, Peg, and his wonderful children, Fred Jr., Ron, Craig, and Karen.

The electric golf cart still works at the farm with Fred W. Marshall's name on the front. The three bedroom trailer, however, is gone.

When Fred purchased the trailer, the owner failed to pay off a lien on the trailer with Fred's hard-earned money. About two years later an arrogant young man with Tennessee plates on his car arrived at the farm. He announced that his company had a lien against the trailer.

He had no compassion for the true story and his only recourse was to repossess the trailer that was now owned by me. I absolutely refused to pay for the trailer twice. He came a few days later and towed the trailer off the farm. I finally gave up chasing the owner for the financial loss. However, anyone reading this book knows that he is a schmuck for deceiving my sick brother Fred.

One of the events of the 1990s was a birthday party I held at the farm on November 7, 1993. The occasion was a celebration of my sixtieth birthday and Aunt Zoe's ninety-first.

Aunt Zoe was one of the first to arrive and the last to leave. She loved the recognition, meeting all of my friends, and showed a keen interest in everything I was doing at the farm. At that time I was building an indoor swimming pool for horses. The cement had just been poured and she was fascinated with my plan to use the pool for year-round training and rehabilitation for the race-horses.

Following my two suicide attempts several relatives rejected me, but never Aunt Zoe. She gave me constant and complete support during my hard road back to acceptance. She always made me feel that I could return to the winners circle of life.

After the party I made a collage of pictures taken at the farm party and sent it to Elmira. She was thrilled with the gift and proudly displayed the collage over her breakfast table and all her visitors had to see it. Following her death, it was the first item I requested. The same collage now hangs in my lounge at the farm and will remain there until my death—a great memory of a great lady.

It is proudly displayed on the lounge wall over the stall name plate of the horse I named after her: *My Aunt Zoe*.

The joint birthday party was also the grand opening of the *People Track*, which surrounds the horse training track. As I mentioned earlier, this was created when we removed the top soil in construction of the horse training track. This was beautiful black top soil without a stone in it. The three-quarter mile *people track* now rests on over five feet of this beautiful soil. If it was excavated and sold for residential use, the value would exceed one hundred thousand dollars. The surface on November 7, 1993, was gravel. This was the first day that guests walked the *people track*. After I gifted the farm to ARISE in 1999, the people track was paved with black top—ten feet wide. Following the gift, I continued to improve the *people track* and have built twenty-two ten-foot benches every one hundred yards adjacent to the track.

As I mentioned earlier in the book, this track is the only one in Central New York where you can walk three-quarters of a mile, rest on a bench every hundred yards, and return to the starting point. This is great for the elderly and people with health limitations.

At this writing, March 1, 2004, this track, in my opinion, is one of the best walks in Central New York. Presently it is featured in our first Foundation program. Starting in May of 2003, we held *Walk & Talk* sessions every Sunday from one to four in the afternoon. This is a program that gives support to people that suffer from depressive illness. Even though I gave the farm away in 1999, I continue to spend my labor and money on improvements.

In January of 1996, I decided that going back to school for a week might give my depression a lift. A world famous course in Equine Reproduction is given every year at Colorado State University in Fort Collins, Colorado. The Equine facility is magnificent, with the Rocky Mountains rising to the sky on the horizon.

The course provided us with the very latest advances in Equine Reproduction. All the students learned how to collect semen from stallions, evaluate and treat semen samples, and inseminate mares—the entire process of artificial insemination.

The head instructor definitely liked his cocktails at the end of each day. Back at the hotel he hosted a two-hour cocktail party every evening. As you all should know, alcohol is a depressant and should be avoided if you suffer from depression. However, social interaction is good for depression. Chatting with Equine enthusiasts from all over the world definitely helped me more than the alcohol hurt me.

The trip to Colorado was a terrific experience and proved to be very beneficial to my breeding program back at the farm, as well as it helped my depression. The lift to my depression unfortunately was only temporary. However, I strongly recommend a trip, doing something completely different, and meeting new people as therapy for depression.

On June 16, 1996, I found out that owning a piece of property can be a liability. At that time, Peter had offered to rent the old farm house to a horseman that drove our horses at nearby Vernon Downs. This was not a great financial arrangement since horse people are always broke and rent for living in the house was never paid.

June 16th was Father's Day, a very hot day at the farm. The tenant invited several of his buddies up to the farm for a cookout and a huge quantity of beer was consumed. Late in the day, with no permission from Peter or me, they all decided to go swimming in a farm pond on the south border of the farm.

Several years previously we had swam in the pond after a day of haying when we were all hot and covered with hay chaff. A small dock was constructed at that time. No one had been in the pond for years. This was because horses were swimming in another pond upstream. The "road apples" would float downstream to this pond, which was called Sweetheart Pond, canceling all desire for a swim. The make-shift dock was never removed.

Apparently one of the horsemen at the party had seen the dock by the water and suggested that everyone go for a swim. One of the guests dove into the water about six inches from the shore and drove his head deep into the mud. When the alcohol wore off the next day he had some neck pain and was taken to the hospital. One of his cervical vertebrae had been fractured, requiring surgery.

Neither Peter nor I would find out about this party for two weeks. Rumors of someone getting hurt at Doc's farm started to get back to us but details were lacking.

After another week of rumors the facts became shockingly clear. Two gentlemen arrived at the farm all dressed up in suits and ties. I get very suspicious when anyone shows up in a suit, white shirt, and tie. My suspicions proved to be valid. When I announced that I was Dr. Marshall, owner of the farms, they presented me with legal documents charging me with negligence contributing to the injury of this drunken horseman. The suit requested two million dollars of compensation for these injuries.

This was a shock and poor medicine for my depression. At the time, the top limit of my liability was five hundred thousand dollars. If the suit was successful the additional liability would wipe out the farm, our home in Fayetteville, the home in Maine, plus our life savings. Getting a good night's sleep suddenly became a problem.

I was insured by a small rural insurance company located in the Mohawk Valley. The company was terrific, defending me and finally received a summary judgment. We won the verdict, but it did cost the insurance company sixteen thousand dollars in legal fees for my defense.

A few months later I had a grand old barn burn to the ground on the farm. I had restored the barn and built fifteen horse stalls on the ground floor. Fortunately all of the horses had been moved out of the barn to the newly constructed swim barn for their daily swim session. I was shredding hay and old paper for stall bedding with a machine powered by a gasoline engine. The engine overheated and burst into flames. In a matter of seconds the shredded hay and paper were on fire and out of control. The only horse remaining in the barn was *JMF's Sam*. I was able to move *Sam* out of the barn before the fire reached the stalls. The firemen were able to save the other barns on the farm, but the hundred-year-old barn was reduced to ashes in just a few hours.

In my seventy years of life I have observed that some people have a predisposition for depressive illness much more than others. This apparently is caused by our genetic makeup, and I am definitely one of those people. We maintain a crust of self control over the underlying despair. When a major adversity or mental trauma enters our lives, the crust is eroded and we fall into depressive illness. Sometimes we heal up the eroded crust and return to normal. During my twenty-three-year bout with the illness, my shield against depression was constantly breaking down, healing back up, and breaking down again. The biggest problem during these twenty-three years was the destruction of my confidence and self-esteem. It was impossible to know in advance how I would feel or be able to function on a future date. It was very hard to make plans for the future. Every day I see people on this same roller coaster. They are typically irritable, constantly complaining about something, often sick, taking medication for many ailments, busy attending doctors appointments, and generally unhappy with their life.

In 1997, I felt my shield protecting me from depression was seriously breaking down. My father, who was my last living parent, and Uncle Fred, the last of that generation, had passed on. The two-million-dollar lawsuit and the fire loss at the farm had taken their toll. Medication and professional therapy were not helping. My future was once again a big worry. I would eventually find a cure, but it would be three years later.

17

My Last Major Depression,
I Hope

There was not a doubt in my mind that in the summer of 1997 I was sinking back down into the pit of despair. It was definitely the onset of a major depression and we all were concerned.

That summer at Squirrel Island, I realized that I was in big trouble and put in a call to my psychiatrist friend, Dr. Lin, at the Mayo Clinic. He phoned in a prescription for Prozac at a local pharmacy in Maine. Furthermore, he indicated that I should contact a psychiatrist when I returned to Syracuse. A quick fix with Prozac was not going to happen.

Upon our return home I called a psychiatrist that was well recommended and started therapy that would continue for the next three years. This was the first time I had seen a female physician. I definitely feel that females are more gifted for this particular profession. This is why the good Lord had women bear children and care for the young.

Due to my history of suicide attempts she immediately admitted me to the local mental facility, *Benjamin Rush*, for observation. Once again I was back in a depressing lockup with all the precautions taken to prevent suicide attempts. I never became suicidal, but my future and the possibility of life-long incarceration was an ever present worry.

Ruth, Cynthia, and Otey took me into the mental facility. The first twenty-four hours I was locked up in a special area for suicide suspects. The conditions were absolutely deplorable and in serious disrepair. There was one patient that was very deranged. It was just this patient and myself in this unit.

It was very traumatic for Ruth, Cynthia, and Otey to leave their husband and father in this awful place. The next day I was transferred to a regular section, but I was still treated like a crazed animal and kept under double locks and constant vigilance. Once again the main concern was to prevent patients from hurting themselves.

Very little effort was made to encourage patients to cling to the gift of life and I never heard of anyone making a complete recovery. I don't remember any effort to strengthen our faith with our creator. Every mental hospital should have a small chapel—I don't even remember seeing one. Spiritual strength is important in surviving this illness. Hopefully a copy of this book, plus news of other survivors, will be available to these patients in the future to help give them hope for complete recovery.

I can't remember exactly how long I stayed at *Benjamin Rush*, but I do remember that they told me that my insurance coverage was exhausted and I had to leave or self-pay, which once again I refused to do. One requirement before discharge was to sign a statement that I was not suicidal and would not be in the future. This obviously was a hedge against possible litigation which was their number-one concern. Reoccurrence of suicidal impulses is common in some patients. If an unstable patient is discharged and attempts suicide, the hospital could face litigation.

I never felt that my incarceration in four different hospitals ever helped me feel better. These facilities are necessary to stabilize suicidal patients, but they are terrible environments to expect a cure for depression. Adding a few animal residents to these hospitals would be a big plus.

Returning home definitely made me feel better. I had no energy or interest in doing anything. Staying in bed or on the couch was my first choice every day. When Ruth would let me, I would stay in bed all day, getting up long enough to have dinner at around six at night.

I remember one day my daughter stopped in and tried to lecture me on snapping out of it, and get going. She felt I was a quitter and was not trying to get better.

Severe depression is almost like being under a general anesthetic. The patient is virtually helpless until improvement is realized.

Asking a despondent patient to get going is like asking someone with a broken leg to enter a foot race. They just can't function.

The next three years were pretty much the same—just trying to survive. Visits to the psychiatrists were frequent and pretty much the same. Ruth always went with me and we had nice visits with the doctor, but no improvement in my despondent spirits. Once again the drugs and dosages were changed frequently in the hopes of finding something that helped. It is amazing to realize the vast number of medications available today to treat patients with depressive illness. I know friends that have struggled with depression for over thirty years and are still trying new drugs in search of a cure.

Pharmaceutical companies are making a fortune coming out with new drugs for depression. There are always millions of patients anxious to try the new medicine, hoping that the new pill will be the one to cure their depression. The new pills often cost between four and five dollars a pill.

My favorite visits to the farm even lost their appeal. Some weeks I never went to the farm at all.

Our family, myself included, started to feel that the farm was too much for me and maybe I should consider selling. Peter, however, loved the farm and was against this suggestion.

I pretty much accepted the fact that the rest of my life would be the same; feeling morose, no energy, frequent visits to the psychiatrist, trying new drugs, changing dosages, and hoping for a cure that probably would never happen.

18

I Gave Away the Farm

For some time I was concerned about the future of the farm. Since 1984, the farm had been my best therapy for depression. The eighty-four acres on the north side of New Boston Road were open fields. Between 1984 and 1997 I made all the improvements that I have mentioned previously.

I always had a dream that in some way the farm would help others suffering from depression as it helped me. Now the illness had eroded my confidence and killed this dream. I knew pursuing this goal would be impossible in my despondent condition.

The thought of my farm growing up to weeds and falling into disrepair haunted me. A ride into the countryside will reveal farm after farm falling into ruin. They all obviously were the pride and joy of their owners who built them, but following generations chose other vocations and the farms died also.

My accountant suggested that I could gift the farm to an existing foundation. The farm would survive and I could realize a tax deduction as a charitable donation, or I could sell it for nearly half a million dollars.

I had became interested in the programs carried out for physically handicapped individuals by the ARISE Foundation in Syracuse. I had viewed a program on television that showed a special ski sled that allowed paraplegics to enjoy downhill skiing. At a meeting in their Syracuse office I shared my dream for the farm. They were impressed.

My melancholic decision to gift the farm was recognized as an unbelievable opportunity to receive a half-million-dollar piece of real estate free by the ARISE director. She was aware of my depressive illness and had previously visited me while I was hospitalized at *Benjamin Rush*. Without questioning the sanity of my decision with my family, she organized a dinner announcing the gift and invited several Syracuse dignitaries. The legal transfer had not been made.

Most of my family questioned my decision, but there was no way I would change my mind after this public announcement. This was definitely a shrewd move by the ARISE executive director.

The closing occurred in July of 1999. I did not attend the legal transfer; shaking hands and having my picture taken. I was home in bed in a despondent state. The farm I created was no longer mine. This deranged decision would prove to be the biggest mistake of my life.

I did, however, retain lifetime use of the eighty-four acres for myself and my son, Peter. A specification in the gift stated that the farm would forever be available for the exclusive use of people with disabilities. Five stalls, two pastures, and four shelters were reserved for our lifetime use and the track could be used by any horseman stabled at the Jim Marshall Farm stable on the north side of New Boston Road.

I still owned one hundred and thirty acres and the original farm buildings on the north side of New Boston Road, but the special part I had developed was gone.

ARISE retained an architect to develop a plan for the farm and I was invited to the first presentation. I was devastated after reviewing the proposal. I voiced my extreme displeasure with the plan. It was my opinion that the plans would ruin the farm. I was never invited to another meeting. It was difficult to realize that although I had created and gifted the farm, I was now ignored and impotent to influence future plans.

My despair prevailed, but a breakthrough was about to happen.

19

Finally A Complete Cure

About three months after the official land transfer to ARISE, Ruth came home with a book about sleep. Ruth is an avid reader, but I am not. She has always been on the lookout for a book that might spike my interest, especially since all I wanted to do was stay in bed.

Throughout my depressive years a good night's sleep was a dream that never came true. My best description of my illness was severe and constant mental fatigue. I seemed to be as tired in the morning as I was the night before. Staying in bed longer or even all day didn't seem to make any difference.

I did get interested in the book and read it cover to cover. It was written by a doctor who had spent a professional lifetime studying patients with abnormal sleep patterns. In the back of the book several sleep centers across the country were listed along with their phone numbers. I called the St. Joseph's Sleep Center in Syracuse and was able to get scheduled for a study. Usually a physician has to make the arrangements, but when I told the girl I was Dr. Marshall she assumed I was an MD and scheduled the sleep study.

Having a sleep study is an interesting experience. About six to eight patients show up at about nine in the evening and are checked into separate rooms, each with a bed and a bath. Once you have your pajamas on, a technician explains the study and attaches many wires to your head and body, including your legs. The leg wire is to detect "shaking leg syndrome" that can be a problem for some patients.

Trying to sleep with all these wires in place is a problem, but almost everyone eventually falls asleep for a short time and that's all they need for the evaluation.

In my own study, mild Sleep Apnea was detected. Sleep apnea is when your airways collapse to some extent during sleep, causing the oxygen requirements to fall below necessary levels. Your brain detects this deficiency and brings you out of the deep REM sleep to a higher level. Your collapsed airway opens, and the oxygen level is restored.

The deep REM sleep is the quality sleep that is most effective in charging the battery. The longer you are in REM sleep, the better the night's rest.

In my case, thirty-two times an hour my brain brought me out of REM sleep to correct the oxygen deficiency. Apparently almost everyone does this maybe two to five times an hour, but some are so bad that it happens about eighty to ninety times an hour. People that are obese have more problems with sleep apnea than slim, fit people. I have always been overweight and fall into the group more apt to have sleep apnea.

The interruptions in sleep can only be detected by one of these studies. You do not actually wake up, and therefore, have no idea it is happening.

A simple remedy for this affliction is to sleep with a C-Pap unit. C-Pap is the abbreviation for Continuous Pulmonary Airway Pressure. This apparatus is a mask that fits snuggly over your nose and is connected by tubing to a small motorized fan that blows room air into your lungs. This machine is adjusted to a pressure sufficient to prevent your sleep apnea.

The other remedy for sleep apnea is surgery. The soft palate relaxation during sleep is often the cause of the apnea. Surgical removal of part of this tissue can be curative. Sometimes just losing your excess pounds can also correct the sleep apnea.

I decided that the C-Pap unit was my first choice. I'd had enough surgery on my poor body already. This required another overnight study using the C-Pap apparatus. Again, trying to sleep with the mask on is difficult, but everyone seems to eventually sleep long enough for the technicians to determine the pressure setting to prevent the apnea. My requirement was ten. Most patients only require a pressure of five, others as high as fifteen.

Initially the best option is to rent the machine, because they are so expensive, to make sure you can accept their use. Most people eventually give up and can't get used to the suffocating feeling that is ever present with the mask on. Also, there is some noise associated with the use that is annoying to your spouse.

I was intrigued with the concept that sleep apnea could explain my constant fatigue. It was difficult for both Ruth and I to adjust to the unit. However, I was determined to give this a lengthy trial period. Ruth wasn't thrilled with the noise, but we had slept together for thirty-nine years and we weren't about to go to separate bedrooms. She was determined to try to adjust also.

The first month this seemed to be a hopeless torture for both of us. It was hard to get used to the suffocating feeling of this mask strapped over my nose. I was getting very little sleep and still felt lousy the next morning. Ruth was also getting fed up with losing sleep as a result of the noise.

However, after about six weeks I started to notice a slight improvement. I think I was starting to get used to this contraption and probably was getting more sleep as a result.

After three months I absolutely knew I was improved. My desire to stay in bed was starting to vanish and I actually had some energy in the morning and started to get out of bed and plan some activity.

After six months I knew I was feeling better than I had in twenty-three years. My depression had lifted. I started to talk to Ruth about being cured of my depression. This was the best news she had heard in a long time. She was not about to complain about the noise. The man she married thirty-nine years earlier had returned from a long absence. Happy days were here again.

My psychiatrist was happy that I was improved, but attributed the change to the medication. I felt cured and felt the psychiatric visits could be terminated. It was a huge boost to my confidence to realize that I could go solo and function without seeing a therapist for the first time in twenty-three years. It was just like the first time I rode a bicycle without training wheels. YES!! I also told Ruth we could use the one hundred and thirty-five dollar cost of these visits for other needs. The psychiatrist advised me to keep seeing her on a regular basis. Finally I agreed we would keep the next visit scheduled for August 2000, but that would be the last. I even wrote final payment on the last hundred and thirty-five dollar check.

When I informed the doctor of my decision and she read the notation on the check, she went ballistic. She predicted that I would relapse in the future and that she might be too busy to see me when that happened. I was very confident of my cure and we parted company. She may prove to be right, but it's been almost four years now and I still feel 100 percent cured.

She is a very nice person, but I wish she had wished me well and asked me to call if I again needed her help.

Why was I better? Utilizing my Veterinary education in Anatomy and Physiology, I have come up with a theory:

The only place in our bodies that oxygen in the air can pass into our blood is the small sacs at the end of the bronchioles in our lungs called alveoli. During sleep many people's breathing becomes very shallow, which minimizes the amount of air that reaches the alveoli. This is much worse if you have sleep apnea.

The C-Pap unit actually blows up your lung like a balloon. This allows much more air to reach the alveoli and a better opportunity for more oxygen to enter the blood stream. This added oxygen for six to eight hours every night refuels our brain

cells and Presto!, the next morning our batteries are fully charged and ready to func-
tion at full capacity for twelve hours.

We all know that oxygen deprivation even for a short time can cause serious brain
damage. Why not fuel our brains overnight with more oxygen? I know this therapy has
helped my son Peter and I. Sleeping with a C-Pap unit would help anyone, if they
could get used to the unit.

Perhaps the miraculous cure that I experienced will not work for others, but
isn't it worth a try? There would be no need to go through the complicated and
expensive sleep study. The depressed patient just needs to start using the C-Pap
unit for a six-month trial period at a pressure of at least ten. Obviously this treatment would have to be monitored by a Pulmonary Physician and a Mental
Health professional. Presently I am trying to arrange at least two of these respective professionals to start a trial study. There are scores of depressed patients that
will be anxious to try the treatment.

Now I was getting back to "full speed ahead," just like my younger days. I was
going to the farm every day and made plans for the future. There was one big
problem; I had given the best part of the farm away.

Now that my brain was working, I started to realize the magnitude of the mis-
taken gift of the farm.

I started thinking of ways to get the farm back. Several letters were written to
the officers and directors of ARISE explaining the mental mistake I had made. I
tried to explain a plan where they could continue to use the farm as in the past.
Ownership would return to me and I would take care of all of the expenses and
maintenance.

When this offer was rejected, I offered to give them fifty acres of prime real
estate on the north side of New Boston Road. I even designed a complete facility
on this parcel and offered to help build it. I desperately needed the race track for
our horse training activities. ARISE planned to build an arena for their activities
that could be built on the fifty acre parcel as well. They didn't need the race track.

ARISE was not about to part with their gifted windfall and all my offers were
rejected.

With my mental health restored, I was not about to give up on my dream of a
Foundation helping people suffering from depressive illness.

My next goal was to try to get half of the farm back, half for ARISE and half
for Jim Marshall Farms Foundation, Inc. This offer was rejected. Finally I scaled
down my request to a few acres on the eastern border of the farm adjacent to the

race track and the People Track. The anticipated mission of my Foundation was closely tied to access to these two tracks that I had constructed.

I even retained a prominent attorney in Syracuse to represent my interests in getting some of the gifted acres for my Foundation. Unfortunately, the attorney turned out to be a close friend of the ARISE Executive Director.

This turned out to be a bad decision. We had one forty-minute meeting arranged by the attorney, but nothing happened. The only result was a drain of twenty-eight hundred dollars in legal fees from my savings account.

Since my relationship with the ARISE executive director was strained, she appointed her friend as an arbitrator to hopefully reach a compromise with our differences. The arbitrator and I met together every week for several months.

Under consideration was my last proposal to transfer a few acres to my yet to be approved Foundation and coexist—both utilizing the facility for our respective missions.

The meetings with the arbitrator were not going well. He constantly described me as a high maintenance individual. He also indicated that if I couldn't become friends with ARISE farm employees, the board would be reluctant to return any part of the gifted eighty-four acres to my Foundation.

I couldn't believe what was going on. Here I was, the largest single benefactor ARISE had ever known (the farm was appraised at half a million dollars), and I was being treated as Public Enemy Number One. They even changed the name of the farm from *ARISE at Marshall Farms* to *ARISE at the Farm*. I will never forget driving by as the executive director's husband painted out *Marshall* on the sign.

Finally the arbitrator reported that he had met with the ARISE Board and if I agreed to certain rules for a period of time they would consider a transfer of seven of the eighty-four acres to my Foundation. He said I would receive a letter shortly with this official decision outlining the rules I had to live by.

On April 15, 2002, I received the following letter:

Joseph M. Snyder, Esq.
5786 Widewaters Parkway
PO Box 3
DeWitt, New York 13214-0003

April 15, 2002

Dr. James O. Marshall, DVM
8122 East Genesee Street
Fayetteville, NY 13066

Re: Access to *Arise at The Farm, Inc.*

Dear Dr. Marshall:

As a member of the Board of Directors of Arise (the "Board"), I have been asked to communicate to you recent Arise Board decisions regarding your use of the farm facility.

Your generosity to our organization has provided us with the infrastructure necessary to help and assist many people with disabilities. As our programs continue to grow in both volume and use, the board feels it is appropriate to designate specific times for access to the facilities that you have lifetime privileges. This is being done to help ensure farm facility safety and eliminate confusion between our activities.

Arise will have exclusive use of the following facilities during the following dates & times:

AREA	DAYS	TIMES
Horse stall area	Monday – Saturday	9am – 6pm
Track & swimming area	Monday – Saturday	9am – 6pm
Kitchen, lounge & office	Monday – Saturday	9am – 6pm

Your use of these areas will be permitted either before or after these hours Monday thru Saturday. You may have access to the facility all day on Sunday, as Arise is closed. These days and times are, however, subject to change as our program needs change.

We trust that you will respect and cooperate with the farm usage timeframes as designated above. Our goals of helping people in need are mutual, and as long as that remains the priority in our respective actions, there is no reason the relationship between you and Arise cannot continue to grow and prosper.

Sincerely,

Joseph M. Snyder

F:\DATA\LEGAL\SNYDER\LETTERS\AriseBoardLetter.doc
4/15/02

I could not believe what I was reading. The restrictions pretty much banished all of us from using the track and farm except on Sundays. I couldn't even go over and check my own horses for nine daylight hours, six days a week. This was a clear violation of the agreed terms at the time of the gift.

The first thing I did was call an attorney I knew in Utica and made an appointment. I wanted to initiate a lawsuit against ARISE at the Farm for two million dollars. This is approximately what it would cost to build another facility to breed and train our horses.

The next thing I did was call the arbitrator and fire him. I informed him that if this order was not negated, I was initiating legal action.

Shortly after hanging up with the arbitrator, I called a reporter I knew with the Syracuse Post-Standard and asked to see her as soon as possible. The next day, after I had cooled off, I shared with her the letter I received and my plan for legal retaliation. Before writing the story she promised to call the President of the Board of Directors and inform him of the pending litigation.

Ten minutes after her call, the President called me and told me to disregard the letter and use the track and farm as we needed. He also returned pasture number three to our exclusive use. He definitely favored peaceful coexistence and definitely wanted to avoid litigation. We arranged a meeting in the near future. The arbitrator was never mentioned.

I can honestly say that this individual avoided a nasty well-publicized lawsuit that would have damaged all of our respective dreams for years.

As of April 19, 2004, when this manuscript goes off to the publisher, the chemistry with ARISE has improved greatly. The Executive Director has resigned and her replacement, Tom McKeown is a terrific man that I get along with very well. The eighth Farm Director, Joe Treglia, also is a great guy that respects me and the magnitude of my gift. We all share a hope for coexistence here at the farm.

The 7.8 eight acres I have requested from ARISE has not yet been transferred. My three-and-a-half-year struggle to get part of the gifted eighty-four acres back needs to be successful. Without the land our programs and plans for the future are up against a stone wall. This decision is up to the ARISE Board of Directors. We all hope and pray for the transfer soon, allowing our mission to go forward. Hopefully I will be blessed with enough years of good health to raise the necessary funding to complete the facility I have dreamed about for years. People with depressive illness will have a refuge to go to, *where animals help people*, together with help from others, classified as *Life Mentors* and *Life Boosters*.

20

The Foundation is Born

During the year of 2000 as I worked my way out of despair, thanks to the sleep therapy, my dream of forming a Foundation helping depressed citizens started to resurface. The farm facility I had constructed for this purpose was no longer mine, but I decided to go ahead anyway. I had the faith that someday this dream of mine could come true.

Vernon Snow, who had coached and encouraged me to start a Foundation, had passed on. I decided to call Ann Scanlon, his very capable, personal secretary for years, to seek some advice. Ann continues to be the secretary for the John Ben Snow Foundation, and Jonathan Snow has succeeded his father as President of the Foundation.

Ann directed me to an attorney in Syracuse that had several not-for-profit Foundations. The goal is to be approved as a 501 (c)(3), Public Charity Foundation. This status allows you to receive tax deductible donations, plus the ability to seek grants from other Foundations.

The attorney informed me that this could be accomplished in nine months at the very most and the cost would not exceed five thousand dollars. Two years later, plus ten thousand dollars in legal fees, on December 16, 2002, we finally received a 501 (c)(3) approved letter from the IRS. We were classified as a Private Operating Foundation. The attorney explained that since I was the sole funder, the IRS required this classification.

This presented one major problem. Every Foundation that I contacted informed me that they would not consider any grants to Private Foundations. I found out that I had to obtain a Public Charity classification. The attorney indicated that this would be another nine months and another five thousand dollars. Probably another two years and ten thousand dollars?

I was shocked! Several wonderful friends were donating fifty and one-hundred dollar gifts. All of their donations and all of my own were used for legal fees. Finally I decided to get on the phone and see what I could do myself. After several referrals, I talked with a real person, not a recording. His name was Paul Kerr who worked in an IRS office in Chicago.

He asked me to send him copies of previous applications and information about the Foundation. I mailed everything I had, plus a video illustrating the *Walk & Talk* programs. Paul called me back after reviewing everything, plus the video, and was impressed with our mission. He led me through the whole process, mailing forms back and forth to Chicago. Within thirty days I received the official letter approving the Public Charity designation to be effective on January 1, 2004, and terminating the Private Operating Foundation on December 31, 2003. All this was accomplished with no cost to our Foundation.

Actually, I found out that I could have applied for the Public Charity designation from the very beginning. The attorney was wrong. Every new Public Charity has to go through a sixty-month evaluation period. At the end of this period you have to prove that 30 percent of the total revenues come from a diverse group of citizens. Each qualified donation cannot exceed two percent of the total five-year accumulated revenues.

My advice to anyone wishing to start their own Foundation: Try to find a well informed IRS agent like Paul Kerr. You will save yourself a lot of money in legal fees.

During the first year the Foundation did not qualify for even one grant because of the *Private Operating Foundation* designation. We did, however, receive fifty-three thousand four hundred and fifty dollars from eighty-seven private donors. The donations allowed us to buy office equipment and supplies to start programs assisting people suffering from depressive illness.

Starting May 4, 2003, we held *Walk & Talk* sessions every Sunday throughout the summer, ending October 26, 2003. I received permission from ARISE to use the farm facility I gifted to them on Sundays from one to four in the afternoon for twenty-six Sundays.

These programs proved to be very successful and several regulars never missed a session, rain or shine. One elderly lady reported the sessions were the highlight of her week and she couldn't wait until Sunday afternoon arrived. She brought her grandchildren on occasion and at least for a couple of hours her depression lifted.

The exposure to all the animals was therapeutic. I called the sessions *Walk & Talks* and we encouraged everyone to walk around the people track and soak up the peace and tranquility of this beautiful rural setting. Over the previous two years I had constructed twenty-two ten-foot benches adjacent to the people track. They are placed about one-hundred yards apart. Anyone with health problems can walk one-hundred yards and rest for a while on a bench. This setup allows them to complete the three-quarter-mile walk and return to the spot they started from.

Everyone attending the *Walk & Talks* received an ID badge with their photo and first name only. A few individuals that I thought were well qualified received special designation as *Life Mentors*.

Many of the *Life Mentors* were survivors of depression like me. We encouraged visitors to take a walk around the people track with a *Life Mentor*. These people are amateur therapists and do a wonderful job explaining the mission of the Foundation and helping others.

The biggest obstacle of our programs is the stigma of revealing one's troubled Mental Health. Many victims feel that attending our *Walk & Talks* will brand them as *wackos*. We constantly encourage everyone to attend these sessions.

Volunteering as a *Life Mentor* can be very rewarding. Realistically, almost all of us need support to get over occasional bumps in the road of life. Bringing your children and grandchildren adds a wonderful dimension of therapy to the programs. Holding a newborn baby, as well as newborn puppies, chicks, bunnies, etc., always brings a smile to the face of the most depressed individuals.

Although many of our *Life Mentors* are experienced and well qualified, we are very quick to inform the public that no one here is certified or licensed in any way to have special expertise in Mental Health therapy. This is to avoid any possibility of litigation. The *Life Mentors* are just good citizens that want to help. Some of them have survived depressive illness themselves. We always recommend people seek professional counseling, and explain that our Foundation presently is just support. Visitors are directed to the yellow pages of the phone book for professional services.

Presently all of our programs are completely free of charge. I hope our Foundation activities can always be free. This may not be possible in the future when our overhead expenses increase, but my hope is to have visits to the farm remain forever free.

Very popular features of our weekly *Walk & Talks* are the horses, the petting zoo, and the carriage rides around the horse track. Our race-horse, *JMF's Sam* is in the main stable, and each Sunday we report how he performed the night before at races held at nearby Vernon Downs. These two horses were born on the farm. Over the last eight years of racing together they have earned over two-hundred and fifty thousand dollars. Most of the farm facility has been built and paid for as a result of their racing success.

We bring in two mares and their foals every Sunday. The foals were both born in April, and the many visitors have been amazed with their growth in six months. The mares and foals also enjoy being therapists to the many depressed visitors.

My first Thoroughbred, *Valiant Valerie VZ*, also greets the visitors. She is a granddaughter of *Seattle Slew* and gets a lot of affection from visitors, which has helped her attitude. Hopefully these young horses will contribute to the Foundation through their future racing success.

My first visit to a psychiatrist for depression in 1977 was thirty-five dollars. My last visit, twenty-three years later in 2000 was one-hundred thirty-five dollars. This one-on-one therapy is just too expensive for the average person. If one or two sessions would affect a cure, the cost would be insignificant. However, depressive illness often continues for years. Only our very wealthy citizens can afford this ongoing expensive therapy. The best insurance coverage only covers a small percentage of the cost.

Accurate surveys of mental illness reveal that of every one-hundred births, one will be a Schizophrenic, one will be Bi-polar (manic depression), and twenty will suffer depression at some time in their lives. Thirty thousand citizens successfully end their lives each year to terminate their suffering from depression. In the year 2000, a study of gun-related deaths revealed ten thousand homicides and sixteen thousand suicides. Six thousand more individuals turned the gun on themselves to end their suffering.

For the rest of my life I will be campaigning for free mental health therapy for all our citizens. If we can afford to send eighty-three billion dollars to help Iraq, we certainly can afford free mental health therapy for our own citizens.

I do not believe in socialized medicine in all medical professions, but Mental Health needs to be addressed differently. It should be free! The qualified therapists will be well-paid government employees.

If we can make the mental health of our citizens the very best in the world, we will always be the best place to live in the world.

In 2003, President Bush appointed Michael Hogan of Ohio to head up Mental Health in our country. At a meeting in Syracuse he described mental health as a program in shambles. I personally agree with him. Over twenty-three years of depression the cost of my own professional therapy would buy a new retirement home on a golf course in Florida. Many victims of depression have paid more. The vast majority of depressed citizens receive little or no therapy at all.

It is my hope that during the remaining days of my life the Foundation I have started will make a difference in some lives. The best legacy I can leave is the creation of facilities across this great country where everyone can receive the very best mental health therapy free of charge.

I'm encouraging everyone reading this book to attend at least one *Walk & Talk*, and then possibly become a regular. Hopefully you will become an advocate for free Mental Health Therapy for everyone, conveying your opinions to our elected officials.

Everyone agrees that our tax dollars should be used to give our youth the best possible Public Education. Shouldn't we extend this obligation to provide free Mental Health Therapy to all our citizens? This will enable them to utilize their education and maximize their abilities and achievements.

The divorce rate will go down. There will be fewer single-parent children in our schools. Workers will be more productive, with fewer sick leaves. Individuals will be able to make better decisions and live happier lives. They will not resort to alcohol and drug abuse for gratification. They will not smoke cigarettes that cause lung cancer. They will not resort to crime and violence to solve their unhappy situations.

I think everyone should assess their mental health. Are you starting each morning with a fully charged battery or are you functioning just well enough to get by?

Since my recovery in 2000, I feel that I'm using close to one-hundred percent of my mental ability. Between 1977 and 2000, I functioned on a fraction of this potential. Some years were better than others, but never one-hundred percent.

During these years I ran a successful veterinary practice, provided for a wife and four children, served as President of Rotary, served on the Board of Examiners for Veterinary Medicine, and contributed to my church and community. If I had found a cure in 1977 instead if 2000, I know I could have done better.

Every day I witness individuals that are operating with less than their full potential, possibly because of a slight depression problem.

Improving our mental health is a challenge for everyone else—not just those that are dysfunctional with depression, suicidal, or incarcerated in mental hospitals. In my opinion, a lot of people can feel better and live more productive lives.

Our wonderful United States of America will be a safer and happier place to live.

21

Summing it Up

Writing this book has brought me a great deal of pleasure and also plenty of pain. Growing up on the farm, my wonderful parents and family, high school, Cornell, my first jobs, and starting my own practice brought back priceless, happy memories. The twenty-three year ordeal with depression, suicide attempts, and the long, hard road to recovery were not pleasant to recall.

Many of my friends and relatives would like me to hush up about my dark days; sweep these memories under the rug and go on with my life now that I have recovered. This revelation may very well adversely affect my popularity and credibility. Anyone who chooses death (suicide) at any time in their life loses acceptability in our society. We all are expected to *snap out of it, pull ourselves up by our boot straps, and overcome our adversity. When the going gets tough, the tough get going.* Anyone who gives up becomes a *wimp* and decides to *check out* with suicide automatically falls to the very bottom class as citizens of our success-oriented society.

However, the reality of this illness is that millions all over the world suffer just as I did. In the United States alone over twenty-nine thousand people successfully end their depression and their lives by means of suicide each year. For every successful attempt, there are one-hundred attempts that fail, like my two attempts. Then, for every one that makes an attempt, there are thousands more that have actually developed a death wish in their lives.

Accurate reports from our precious teenagers in this country have revealed that one out of every four have considered suicide as a viable solution to life's problems at one time in their young lives.

During the first forty-three years of my life suicide was an absolute impossibility. I was happy, full of energy, and attaining every goal I set for myself. If anyone had predicted my downfall to suicide, myself, and anyone else who knew me, would write them off as crazy.

Suicide is often described as *a permanent solution to a temporary problem.* I can assure you from personal experience that victims of lengthy depression view suicide as *a permanent solution to a permanent problem.* No one will terminate their life if they know that recovery is possible. I want to prove to these victims that recovery is possible, even if it takes twenty-three years. Constant support is a necessity for recovery. This is the mission of my Foundation.

Most people believe, as I do, that our creator has a plan for our lives. The miraculous way that I survived was a strong message that compelled me to write this book and start the Foundation to help others.

My best description of depression is that of a big sink-hole in the middle of the road of life that many of us stumble into at one time or another. Some fall into this pit at a very young age. The incidence of depression in our teenagers is increasing at an alarming rate.

I was forty-three years old when I first became trapped in this pit. The older I get the more I am convinced that almost everyone will fall into this hole at one time or another before they reach the finish line. My father was the most energetic, positive, success-driven individual I have ever known. A stroke destroyed even his wonderful enthusiasm for life. He expressed this to me in his own words, *Jim, its' planting time for your dad.* He wanted to give up on life and die; a major symptom of depression. He lived almost eighty years before slipping into this dark hole.

Many fall in for a few days and jump right out. The problem arises when we are unable to get out for long periods of time. We climb up the slippery sides of the pit and then slide back down, unable to get out completely. Fortunately, very few fall to the very bottom of this hole and become suicidal as I did, but many are unable to get out completely for years. I was trapped in this sinkhole for twenty-three years, climbing up the sides and slipping back down, unable to get out and jump back on the happy, healthy road of life. I was suicidal for only a short time in 1985, but complete recovery did not occur until 2000.

The main reason for this book and the Foundation is to hopefully help others mired in the sinkhole of depression for long periods of time. I was hospitalized in four different mental health facilities. During this time I never met anyone who recovered completely and got back on the happy road of life. If a similar life story was available back then, maybe I could have braved the storm and resisted the suicidal impulses. A complete recovery at that time seemed impossible. I'm sure thousands have completely recovered, but very few want to tell the world their story. Stories of recovery from auto accidents, plane crashes, avalanches, sinking boats, fires, cancer, heart attacks, and other causes are very popular. Surviving suicidal depression, forget it!

If this book and my Foundation prevent the loss of one precious life by suicide it will be well worthwhile.

Curing a major depression is not a simple task. The good Lord has created us all a little different. What works for me may not help you. Unfortunately, there is no therapist so gifted that can pull you out of this pit in one visit or even scores of visits. Likewise, there is no one magic pill that will work for everyone either. As I have mentioned earlier, I have had twenty-five different prescriptions for depression over my twenty-three years of therapy. However, I want everyone to know that if I made it, so can you. It may take years of professional therapy, medication, and support to finally get out of this sinkhole. I hope this book, my Foundation, and visits to the farm will help.

It is very easy to recognize someone with a broken bone. They have a big cast that tells everyone that they are injured. Spotting a person suffering from depression is very difficult. I personally ran a successful Veterinary practice for many years when I was depressed. My suicidal attempt was a shock to almost everyone that knew me. It is a very secretive illness. Even visits to therapists are closely monitored to prevent recognition. Most waiting rooms are partitioned so that patients waiting to enter never see those patients exiting. There is way too much shame associated with this illness. A prominent symptom is withdrawal from others, even good friends, when just the opposite would be therapeutic.

If you visit a *Walk & Talk* session at the farm you will be hard pressed to tell the difference between those suffering from depression who are seeking support, and the participants that are there rendering their support.

This book has already touched the life of a beautiful twenty-one-year-old that showed absolutely no signs of a depressive illness. I had hired her to type my manuscript onto a computer disk that the publishers require. She has done a terrific job typing my handwritten words on a disk. One day after completing most of the book, she called me, very distraught, asking if she could talk with me. She had struggled with a depressive illness with frequent crying spells for five years and kept it a secret, not even telling her mother. Typing the story of my life had convinced her to confess her illness and talk with me. She had even contemplated suicide.

At that time a part-time job opened up at the farm caring for the horses. I offered the job, but also recommended professional therapy. I always suggest an MD and medication first, and the farm and the animals as additional therapy.

The combination worked wonders and she returned to her outgoing, vivacious self quickly. She is now one of our *Life Mentors* and is helping other young gals with depression. Helping others will prevent a relapse.

Supporting someone with a similar illness is very therapeutic. When you make someone else feel a little better you will find that you will feel better. There will always be someone worse off than yourself to help.

This belief gave birth to the theme of the Foundation: *When you help someone you help yourself.*

Humor is also terrific therapy for depression. It is impossible to laugh hard and be despondent at the same time. Telling a good joke is actually more therapeutic than listening to one.

Will I slip back into the sinkhole of depression? The last psychiatrist I saw predicted that I would. Only time will tell. The formation of this Foundation to help others, plus the use of the C-Pap unit every night is the therapy that I am sure will prevent a relapse. I feel that I am cured.

My advice to anyone suffering with depression:

1. Find a Mental Health Professional you like

2. Have a brain scan

3. Have a sleep test

4. Reach out for all the support you can get, for example, visiting ou farm or other support groups.

Don't suffer for twenty-three years like I did. Maintain your hope for a complete cure, and never give up!

As I approach my seventieth birthday, I am convinced that every one of us is qualified to be a therapist. Helping others feel better is the secret to getting back on the happy road of life and avoiding future sinkholes that may lie ahead.

Presently it is the spring of 2004 when my manuscript is being mailed to the publisher. I have enjoyed eighteen years of life so far since the time I chose to end my suffering. Although I live each day with constant pain, I have been blessed with the time and opportunity to help others find help and hopefully a complete cure for depressive illness.

Ruth and I live a simple, very enjoyable rural life. I leave the house about 7:30 every morning, seven days a week, stop at the *Hamlet* for a cup of coffee and local gossip, and then proceed on to the farm. I feed all the horses every morning and if anyone could hear me talking to all the horses as they get their breakfast, I would be qualified as a *wacko*.

Only time will tell how successful my Foundation dreams will be. You now have an understanding of the first seventy years of my life. If I live long enough, I might even write another book, *JMF Revisited*. This would be a great way to tell you if my dreams come true.

I started this book with the specific purpose of educating the reader about depression and motivating them to help others that are suffering. Hopefully my story will help remove the shroud of shame and secrecy that envelopes this illness. Once a victim can reveal this affliction and seek help and support, recovery can begin. I hope many of you will join me in this noble mission. Helping someone climb out of this hopeless pit of despair can be a great personal achievement.

For as long as the good Lord will let me live I will be committed to the mission of the Foundation. I hope and pray that I can see some progress in my lifetime curing depression. I have chosen this effort to be my legacy. The transition from despair to hope and happiness in many lives will be my reward.

I would like to conclude my life story with the final words of that wonderful song that Jimmy Durante sang so well:

> *Make someone happy!.........*
> *Make just one someone happy!.........*
> *And you will be happy too!*

Epilogue

I am fully aware that this book and the Foundation will be controversial. There is still a large segment of our society that has little compassion for victims of mental illness, especially when they choose death (suicide). However, when depression and suicide claim the precious life of a close relative or friend this passive attitude changes dramatically. It is replaced by a keen interest in programs to prevent this horrible tragedy.

When I received the 501 (c)(3) approval in December of 2002, I immediately mailed out nearly five hundred announcement letters and brochures to relatives, friends, and colleagues. I selected only those I knew about my age who have been successful and might consider a charitable tax-exempt donation to the Foundation. I avoided all younger families who still had college expenses ahead of them. Most (ninety percent) have made no response.

The ten percent that have responded sent wonderful letters of encouragement and donations that ranged from fifty dollars to twenty-thousand dollars. These individuals will always be very special to me and have strengthened my will to forge ahead with this major undertaking at my rather advanced age.

I have included the following letter of how to become a *Life Booster*.

Jim Marshall Farms Foundation, Inc.
1978 New Boston Road
Chittenango, New York 13037
Phone: (315) 687-5064
Fax: (315) 687-5071
Website: www.JMFFinc.org

JMF Life Boosters

All donations of any amount are helpful and appreciated. Donations have ranged from $50.00 to $20,000.00. Hopefully some of you will choose to become JMF Life Boosters: your yearly contributions can accumulate to reach this level. All donations are deductible (state and federal).

Since I have an admiration for harness horse achievement, I have chosen the following levels for contributions. These reflect race times (for the mile) that we strive for in our equine athletes (harness horses—not thoroughbreds).

1:55 is a very commendable performance. 1:46 is the fastest time ever recorded for a harness horse. 1:45 is a goal that may or may not be reached in the future and, therefore, is the very top level of giving.

Each year we hope our horses reach new levels of performance. Likewise some of you may wish to raise your level as the years go by. We hope to convince you of the very helpful benefit that our programs will have on certain lives. You will be kept informed twice a year by a newsletter. (June and December)

JMF Life Booster Level		Contribution
1:55	(two stars)	$1,000.00
1:54		$2,000.00
1:53		$3,000.00
1:52		$4,000.00
1:51	(three stars)	$5,000.00
1:50		$6,000.00
1:49		$7,000.00
1:48		$8,000.00
1:47		$9,000.00
1:46	(four stars)	$10,000.00
1:45	(five stars)	$20,000.00 or higher

Ruth and I have qualified at the 1:45 level by starting the Foundation. Anyone joining us at this level will be invited once a year to the annual meeting of the JMF Foundation. This will usually be held at Squirrel Island, Maine, an absolutely beautiful spot to visit in July and August. The lobsters here are the best in the world!

We have *Walk & Talk* sessions every third Sunday from 1 to 3 P.M., year round at the farm. You will interact with lots of animals and people (some seeking support—others here to offer their own support). Our motto is: "When you help someone you help yourself."

You also will have an opportunity to take a carriage ride around the horse track (weather permitting).

Depression is much more prevalent than most people realize (especially in our youth). My plan is to offer an option that presently does not exist.

Thank you in advance for considering a tax deductible donation, and I hope to see you some Sunday at the farm to "Walk & Talk."

Sincerely,
James O. Marshall, DVM

My big sister, Ada May Marshall Fearon, was the very first I heard from. She sent a very large check and a letter that I will always treasure. My other sister, Irish twin Zoe, and her husband, Ed, also sent a wonderful note and the largest contribution to date, joining Ruth and I at the *Life Booster* 1:45 level. Our niece and nephew, Bob and Sally Watts, donated at the 1:49 level, and former clients, Maury and Joan Pomfrey at 1:51. Several reached the 1:55 level, such as good friends Skip and Barbara Obold, George and Rita Soufleris, fellow horseman Lon Frocione, fellow horsewoman Muriel Diescher, Leo Eisner, Ed and Joan Tracy, Alex Bennett, Brooksley Born, Dolores Card, Wendy Jefferis, and Veterinarians Dr. Robert Lynk, Dr. Ed Chapman, Dr. Jay Hyman, Dr. Francis H. Fox, and Dr. Ed Leonard.

Jay Hyman is a fellow 1957 classmate at Cornell. He is a major benefactor of our Veterinary College and a survivor himself. He should write his own book of his exciting life, especially surviving a horrific plane crash.

I have written earlier in this book of Dr. Fox. He is probably the Veterinarian I most admire and his large contribution and support of my endeavor was just overwhelming.

The one thousand dollar donation that brought tears streaming down my face was from our daughter, Cynthia. I pay Cynthia a thousand dollars a year, on her birthday, to do the book work for our horse farm. She donated every penny of her year's salary to help her Dad's dream come true.

Other Veterinarians sending large contributions were Bob and Helen Kirk, Bruce Widger, Victor Rendaro, Dick Grambow, Don Fox, Al Ahearne, and Willard Daniels, my terrific former boss from Guilford, Connecticut.

I received letters of support from the present Dean of the Veterinary College, Dr. Donald Smith, former Dean, Dr. George Poppensiek, and Dr. Bob Manning.

Former SAE fraternity brothers at Cornell sending donations were Lee Fingar, Norm Geis, Don Huene, Reverend John Bartholomew, and Bob Hampson. Tom Itin, who I had not spoken with since college, surprised me with a call wishing me well.

Good friends from Squirrel Island, Maine, sending significant donations were Alexander Bennett and Brooksley Born, John and Judy Danforth, John and Jean McIlwain, Phebe Miller, Mitch and Cheeky Draper, Richard and Mary Thomas, Jim and Janet Sheppard, Pat Harrison, Krista Garrison, and George and Ann Spaeth.

Fellow golfers from the Calvary Club sending nice checks were Bob Hall, John Kinsella, Tom Kinsella, Pat and Jerry Edsell, Jim D'Amico, Paul Bihuniak, and Al Curtis.

My largest benefactor from Chittenango was Kenny Carman. Sitting at the counter at the local diner, The Hamlet, one morning I handed Ken one of our new Foundation brochures. He scanned the brochure for a minute, reached for his checkbook, and wrote out a big check. What a guy!! I call Kenny, *number one in Chittenango*.

Other friends with notable donations were Chuck and Kathy Elliott, Mike and Gail Foreman, Sam and Aggy Chase, Tom and Sally Hall, Ann Bryant, my broker at AG Edwards Randall Powers, Dan and Joan Kinsella, David and Alice Firley, Bill and Lois Applegate, Clark and Nancy Mercer, Dick Baldwin, Dick and Nancy Almond, Sue Rank, Nancy Nelson, Michael and Susan Delahanty, Maudie Ritchie, Thomas and Mary Ryan, Garrit and Joan Lugthart, William Hutchens, Aunt Lillian Albertson, Richard Cole, Richard Almond, Richard Baldwin, Christine Gehringer, Peter and Patricia Stucker, Tracey Brant, Willard and Barbara Lipe, Pat and Louise Jerome, Norma Kelley, and Aunt Hannah Jacobsen.

Private contributions are essential to the Foundation existence. We have cut our overhead to the bone, utilizing mostly volunteers. The exposure of people to animals makes our insurance costs horrendous. Unfortunately, the fear of litigation in this day and age has taken a lot of fun out of life and terminated a lot of very worthwhile programs. Hopefully we can survive. A successful multi-million-dollar law suit against the Foundation would definitely terminate our existence. That would be extremely sad!!

All contributions, big and small, are appreciated and continue the mission of my Foundation hopefully for years to come and long after I am gone. We keep careful records of all donations, which can add up over the years, to recognize the donor as a *JMF Life Booster*.

The donors can reach the first *Life Booster* level by donating a hundred dollars a year for ten years. They also can do this with fifty dollars for twenty years, but I doubt I will be here to congratulate them when they reach the 1:55 level.

You may also wish to make a donation dedicated to the memory of a friend whose life was claimed by a depressive illness.

At the present time, I have plans to have *Walk & Talk* sessions every third Sunday of each month, year round, from one to three in the afternoon at the farm to support anyone with depressive illness. Everyone visiting the farm will get the following information sheet:

GENERAL INFORMATION

Welcome to this beautiful farm facility and our Walk & Talk programs. These sessions will be held from 1 to 3 p.m. the third Sunday of each month. We depend on tax-exempt donations, however, donations are optional.

These sessions are not entertainment for the general public (not like the State Fair). Everyone attending is encouraged to wear an ID badge as a JMF Booster or as a Life Mentor. You are expected to be supportive of our mission, which is helping people feel better. This can include your whole family.

You may be attending for support of your own depressive illness, or that of a family member or friend. Others will be visiting to volunteer their support for those seeking support.

If you would like to participate in future sessions we would like you to wear an ID badge at each visit. The badge will have your photo and first name only. (Simply make this request during your visit.) You will then be identified as a JMF Booster. If you have an interest in receiving the additional designation as Life Mentor, please make this request for approval.

Please treat all animals at the farm with kindness and respect at all times. All animals at the farm have good temperaments, but it is important to understand that any animal can be unpredictable if provoked.

Insurance Requirements:

1. No dogs allowed

2. No alcoholic beverages

3. No smoking in any barn

Program Requirements:

1. Wear an ID badge at all times

2. Stay on the people track at all times

3. Enter the horse track for carriage rides <u>only</u> at the two designated locations

If you find these sessions helpful or have suggestions for improvement please write:
Dr. Jim Marshall
JMFF Inc.
1978 New Boston Road
Chittenango, NY 13037
Phone: (315) 687-5064
Fax: (315) 687-5071
Website: JMFFinc.org
Email: jmffinc@hotmail.com

Our programs are a support for depressive illness and not a substitute for professional counseling. Since medication is an important help in the treatment of depression, working with an MD is essential.

Thank You,

James O. Marshall, DVM

Our Mission
Jim Marshall Farms Foundation, Inc.
<u>"Where animals help people"</u>

The most tragic occurrence that can happen in our lives is to lose a child, relative, or friend to suicide. This leaves us with a lifetime of wondering what we could have done to save this precious life. The Jim Marshall Farms Foundation, Inc. is established to provide support for people suffering from depression. The farm is a refuge from their troubles and a place where you are greeted with a friendly smile, a kind word, and the unconditional love that animals can provide.

James O. Marshall, DVM

Dr. Marshall was born and grew up on a dairy farm in Munnsville, New York. His love of animals led him to pursue a career in Veterinary Medicine—graduating from Cornell in 1957.

He started the Fayetteville Veterinary Hospital in 1963 and treated farm animals and companion pets for the next 30 years.

In 1984 he purchased the Taylor Farm in North Chittenango, built the main stable and 5/8 mile track to pursue his interest in Standardbred race-horses.

A depressive illness starting in 1977 clouded his life for the next 23 years. As a result, he sold his Veterinary practice in 1990 and gifted 84 acres of the farm to ARISE in 1999 for the exclusive use of people with disabilities. Those 84 acres are now named "Arise at the Farm." You may wish to read Dr. Marshall's autobiography, <u>Where Animals Help People</u>.

The Story Behind the Dream

During his twenty-three-year battle with depression, Dr. Jim Marshall found the peace and tranquility of the farm, together with the presence of the animals to be very effective therapy. During this terrible time in his life, he miraculously survived two suicide attempts.

In the year 2000, he completely recovered and decided to form a foundation that would utilize this beautiful environment to assist others suffering from this devastating disease.

Depression and the resulting thoughts of suicide are extremely high in our teenage population. Our goal here is to rekindle happiness and the recognition of the gift of life that everyone should enjoy. The wonderfully therapeutic environment and the friendship of JMF Boosters, Life Mentors, and many animals await you at the farm: "<u>where animals help people</u>."

Programs

ARISE at the Farm has agreed to allow JMFF, Inc. to use the existing facilities, that were donated by Dr. Marshall, on Sundays to start Foundation programs for depressive illness.

Walk & Talk sessions utilizing the people track are planned to be held from one to three in the afternoon, the third Sunday of each month. We have several different horsedrawn carriages that will provide rides on the horse track during this time.

ARISE at the Farm expects to allocate a portion of the farm to the JMF Foundation for construction of its own facility, allowing us to function every day and add many more programs. We continue to seek the support of volunteers and donations.

When the facility is completed, the programs for the disabled (ARISE at the Farm), plus those for the depressive illness (JMFF, Inc.) will complement each other. These two foundations working side by side will offer a terrific opportunity for assistance to our troubled citizens here in Central New York.

JMF Boosters

JMF Boosters include anyone of any age who wants to contribute to the foundation financially (optional) and/or as a volunteer, visit the farm and be willing to help others they meet here who may be struggling with life's problems.

All JMF Boosters will be identified with an ID badge. We hope these individuals will enjoy participating in our Walk & Talk programs around the track and realize: "when you help someone, you help yourself."

JMFF, Inc. is an approved 501(c)(3) not for profit foundation that could not exist without the generosity of our supporters and volunteers.

Life Mentors

Over the years, Dr. Marshall has known several individuals he feels have the God given ability to touch lives with love and understanding. He wishes to designate them as Life Mentors. These people are all ages and some of them have had personal experience with depression in their own lives or in the lives of their loved ones. These good citizens have volunteered their time to be Life Mentors at the farm. We do not present them as experts, just good citizens that are willing to help others.

Our program requires that all contact and communication with visitors occur at the farm facility. You will recognize a Life Mentor by the ID badge they will wear.

We hope your visit is enjoyable and beneficial!!!!!

PLEASE READ BEFORE FARM VISIT

An understanding of risk of injury—liability and litigation for claims

We have made every effort to make this farm visit for you and your family as safe as possible.

The farm environment, involving several visitors with close proximity to many different animals, farm equipment, horse carriage rides, horseback riding, and other activities can expose visitors to possible injury.

If this exposure concerns you, we ask that you kindly leave the farm. If you stay and elect to visit again in the future, and we hope you do, you must personally accept all involved risks during your visit and hold harmless all officers, directors, and employees of ARISE at the Farm and Jim Marshall Farms Foundation, Inc.

You will, however, be legally responsible for any damage or injury that you or anyone in your company causes during your visit.

Thank you for this understanding!

———————————————   ———————————————

Joe Treglia   James O. Marshall, DVM

Director of ARISE at the Farm   President, Jim Marshall Farms
                                                                     Foundation, Inc.

As soon as possible, following the anticipated transfer of a few of the eighty-four acres that I gifted to ARISE in 1999, I plan to develop the site. Two buildings are planned.

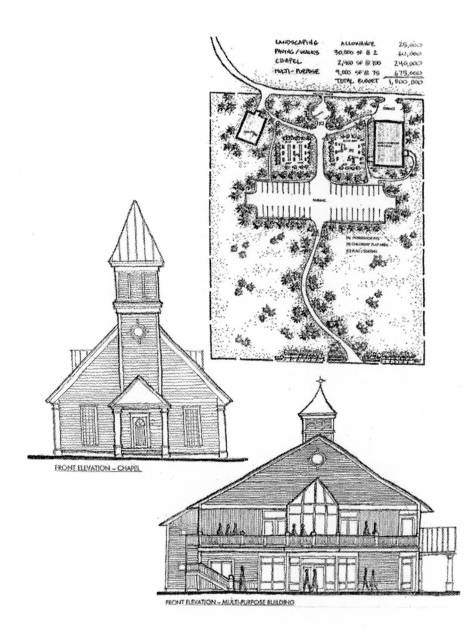

FRONT ELEVATION – CHAPEL

FRONT ELEVATION – MULTI-PURPOSE BUILDING

One is a multi-purpose building adjacent to the people track. The first floor will have offices, a meeting room, kitchen, and a large area of tables for lunch, playing cards, or just conversation. A few treadmills will also be in this area to keep people in shape when the weather is bad outside. The front will open onto a terrace with umbrella tables overlooking the track and horse paddocks in the infield. The west entrance will be private, opening into a reception area and four small rooms for one-on-one counseling.

The second story of this building will be one large room for banquets and receptions. This will also open onto a large outside deck with a spectacular view of the track and horse pastures.

The other building is a New England-style Chapel. I developed this idea from the Chapel on Squirrel Island, Maine. It will be non-denominational with Sunday services, each given by a minister of different faiths. Since a strong spiritual faith is so important in surviving depression, I wanted a Chapel present at the farm. It will be open at all times and located adjacent to the people track.

I plan to dedicate the multi-purpose building to the memory of Dr. Donald Delahanty, whose life was claimed by a depressive illness in 1975. His entire family has been contacted and given me the approval and gratitude to do this. Over a twenty-five year span, Dr. Delahanty contributed to the education of over twelve hundred Veterinarians at Cornell who now have completed very successful careers in our great profession. I am confident that his former students will honor his memory and contribute sufficient funds to build and maintain this building.

The loss of life that often terminates depressive illness is a terrible anguish for friends, relatives, and acquaintances that remain. Supporting a Foundation that is dedicated to healing those afflicted with this terrible illness before it is too late should be an option that many will choose to remember these victims.

The Chapel will hopefully be built and endowed with multiple donations in memory of victims of depression. Presently we have plans to memorialize these victims with special plaques in the Chapel.

Please contact me personally if you would like to remember a friend or relative with a significant donation that can be used in constructing and maintaining the Chapel.

When you consider that we lose ten times the number of our citizens to suicide each year that we lost in the World Trade Center tragedy, something should be done.

Let's accept the challenge to make our citizens' Mental Health the best in the world. The eradication of depressive illness, especially in our youth, allowing them to realize their full potential, will be a terrific investment to secure our future success in the world community. Let's make this our number one goal.

The cost of developing and dropping one mega bomb on Saddam Hussein's palace in Iraq would cover all the antidepressant medication purchased in New York State for six months.

We are the wealthiest country in the world and investing in programs to eradicate depression and suicide are just as important as those to eliminate terrorism.

How can we maintain our position in the world in the future if one out of four teenagers has considered suicide? The mental health of our citizens, especially our youth, is the greatest asset we have to insure the future success and prosperity of our United States of America.

If this book, the Foundation facility, and the farm visits are helpful to you, a friend, or a loved one, please send us your comments, suggestions, and donations. Thank you in advance for all the support you can give.

Dr. Jim Marshall
Jim Marshall Farms Foundation, Inc.
1978 New Boston Road
Chittenango, New York 13037
Phone: 315-687-5064
Fax: 315-687-5071
Email: jmffinc@hotmail.com
Website: www.jmffinc.org

An Addendum to Chapter 15

♦

My Equine Therapists

Horses are very effective therapists. They understood my pain and always found a way to make me feel better with their unconditional love. Somehow I knew they wanted me to cling to life and resist the suicidal impulses that depression created in my sick brain. They probably saved my life.

Telling you about all my Equine Therapists is almost another book. I didn't want to write another book so I added to my autobiography.

My advice to anyone in need of joy in their life, "get a horse!"

Now I'll tell you about my favorite therapists.

National Star

I have written about *Star* earlier in the book as the first horse to set foot (4 feet) on the farm. The termination of the partnership which resulted in his exit from the farm has previously been told. This occurred at the rock bottom period of my depression—only a short time before my first attempt to end my life.

In spite of my despair and loss of interest in anything, I always kept tabs on *Star's* races and location.

He ended up in claimers and his owners and location changed frequently. When I flew to New York City and had some extra time, I would go over to the Meadowlands where he was stabled and look him up. I always found him standing in the very back of the stall in an obvious despondent state. When he heard my voice he would come over to the stall door, obviously delighted to see me. Then, in his own horse way of communication, he would beg me to take him home to the farm. Saying goodbye and leaving him in that stall brought tears to my eyes. As I sit here writing about these meetings I find tears welling up in my eyes again. I honestly was in love with *Star*.

After a few short years, *Star's* performance was starting to fade. Competition at the New York Tracks is fierce, attracting the very best horses racing for the top purses in the country. Following a poor performance, I called the trainer and offered three-thousand dollars to buy him back. The owner wanted ten-thousand—NO DEAL! A couple weeks later, after another poor performance, I called the trainer with the same offer and added: "If you arrange the sale, you'll receive three pictures of Ben Franklin as a personal bonus." He agreed to talk to the owner.

The next day he called to say, "Come and get him, but I really need five pictures of Ben Franklin under the table." There isn't a horse trainer in the world that doesn't light up with an offer of a picture of Ben Franklin, but if some of you readers have led a more sheltered life: A picture of Ben Franklin is a hundred dollar bill!

Karl Lowes, a fellow horseman, drove down to New Jersey with me to pick up *Star*. It was a happy reunion, and this time I didn't have to leave him in that dark stall and say goodbye. *Star* was coming home. It was September 4, 1988.

Back at the farm, *Star* continued to race at Vernon Downs and also enjoyed his role as a stallion. He was a regular and well known at the local track. He was not a frequent winner, but his great desire resulted in a lot of seconds and thirds, along with a nice check for his owner. Most horses reach their peak performance at four to six years of age. *Star* was ten years old in 1991 when he recorded his career best mile at Vernon when he won in 1:56:2. The next year, the wear and tear of racing had taken its toll. He raced nine times and made seventy dollars. It was time to retire. His lifetime efforts had won $48,261.

A Standard-bred stallion is evaluated on the racing achievement of his offspring. *Star's* offspring were not spectacular. For some reason, almost all of his offspring were fillies (females). He had only one colt (male) that was born deformed and had to be put to sleep. If he had had the opportunity to mate with mares of excellent breeding, he might have been a great stallion. However, at JMF, this did not occur.

Probably his very best offspring was *JMF's Jenny. Jenny* was the result of a breeding of *Fancy Horace*, an unraced trotting bred mare. *Star* was a pacer and pacing stallions are always bred to pacing mares. I ignored this rule due to economics—I had the mare and the stallion and the results was *JMF's Jenny*, named after my daughter Jennifer.

Jenny raced four years—1988 to 1991 and made $15,476. Her best effort was winning at Vernon in 159:2, which at one time was considered a great achievement, but not anymore. *Jenny's* claim to fame was as a broodmare. When mated to *Romantic Prince*, a stallion stabled at the farm, she produced *JMF's Sam* and later *JMF's Sammy. JMF's Sammy* (named after my oldest grandson) was sold and was somewhat successful, but *JMF's Sam* (named after my son in law, Sam Vulcano) proved to be a big winner and by far the most successful offspring of *Romantic Prince*. *Sam* is still racing and has made over $125,000.

Star's other offspring that did make the races were *JMF's Josie* (named after Josie Vulcano) and *JMF's Cindy* (named after my daughter Cynthia).

Both *JMF's Josie* and *JMF's Cindy* were pullers and very hard to control. A puller is a horse that has a hard mouth. Pulling back on the reins attached to the bit in the mouth usually slows the horse down. A puller is hard to slow down no matter how hard you try to draw back on the reins. *Star* himself was a puller, but *Cindy* and *Josie* were even worse. Other horsemen are always offering advice on ways to handle problem horses. One day at Vernon they were schooling horses behind the new Cadillac starting gate. A fellow horseman told me to drive *Josie* right into the starting gate and let the gate stop her. *Josie* hit the gate at about thirty miles an hour and almost wrecked the new Cadillac starting gate. I was informed to never bring *Josie* back to the track. *Josie's* career was over, winning only $1,944—hardly enough to pay her feed bill.

JMF's Cindy also had a feisty temper (like her namesake), and was hard to handle. I sold her to a horseman in Maine and she had a fairly successful career racing in Maine.

Star's retirement at the farm continued until 1997 when my depression worsened and I was unable to get to the farm on a regular basis.

A fellow horseman convinced me that I had to clean house and sell all of my old, favorite retired horses to the Amish to finish their careers pulling buggys in Pennsylvania. It was a sad day when they all left. I couldn't say goodbye. I was home in bed in a despondent state. Now that I am recovered, I would give anything to get *Star* back home if he is still alive. He has a white star on his forehead and four white feet. His lip tattoo is 99682 and would now be twenty-two years old.

JMF's Misty—JMF's Jamie

As previously mentioned, these two colts were the first born on the farm and named after two girls that I met at the Mayo Clinic. They both were born late—June 7, 1988 for *Jamie* and June 21, 1988 for *Misty*. Since all standard-breds become a year older on January 1st each year (regardless of when they were born) we try to plan their births as early in the year as possible. This way a foal born in February is much bigger and stronger than one born in June. This can make a big difference in their abilities racing in their first year as two-year-olds.

When I purchased the two mares at the auction, their predicted foaling date in June made them less attractive to buyers, and therefore I was able to purchase them cheap. Beside the lower value of the foal, born in June, prospective buyers are suspicious that the mares may be difficult to get pregnant. The breeding season in standardbreds ends on July fifteenth each year. Obviously *Bewitching Labell*, dam of *JMF's Jamie* conceived the previous year near the deadline. The gestation period (time pregnant) in horses is eleven months.

Jamie and *Misty* growing up on the farm were terrific therapy for my depression. I would sit on the deck, often in the evening, watching the sun go down together with the two colts frolicking in the paddock. Witnessing this miraculous gift of life in these foals was a delightful factor later in my life in offering this environment to others with depressive illness.

The constant running and playing in the large pasture was a great foundation for their athletic ability. Actually they became really wild and were a real challenge to catch and start training as yearlings.

In October of 1989, I received a call from a gentleman in Canada inquiring about *Bewitching Labell*. One of her previous offspring had been very successful racing in Canada. He wanted to buy the mare. I told him the mare was not for sale but I would consider selling her yearling colt. After some negotiating, a price of eight-thousand dollars was agreed upon—provided I could keep *Jamie* for a few weeks when a trucker could pick him up.

When the buyer arrived I was presented with eighty one-hundred dollar bills. After they left we spread all the bills on a table and took pictures. This seemed to be a wonderful business—very lucrative! That was fifteen years ago and I have never been that fortunate since. The sale of *JMF's Jamie* was beginners luck!

JMF's Misty was my first experience in breaking a colt. He proved to be a real challenge—even for experienced horsemen that were helping me. Speed was not a problem—control definitely was! Every horseman had a different idea about what to do. The more severe the driving bit, the worse he got. Finally, in desperation, I decided to use my own instincts and start over with a very simple driving bit. *Misty* did start to calm down, but was no angel.

The most fun I can remember in those morose days was racing *Misty* at the many fairs in New York State, all of which had harness horse competition. My son Peter and I would arrive at each fairground and immediately look for a strong fence we could tie *Misty* to.

While tied to this fence, we would harness *Misty*, hook up the racing sulky, and then I would get on the seat all ready to go. Peter would then turn *Misty* loose from the fence and off we would go. I never tried to stop him until after the race when he was pooped. At most fairs he was easily the best. Following the starting gate away, *Misty* would go right to the front and would usually win wire to wire. After the race, Peter and I would visit the fair, stuff ourselves with chicken barbeque, and then pick up our winning check before heading home. The check was almost always for over a thousand dollars.

Although *Misty* was a late foal, being born June twenty-first, he was the only offspring of *Brand New Fella* that achieved a two-minute record as a two-year-old. The late Larry Lanterman was the driver on that occasion. Larry was a terrific horseman and friend who was instrumental in starting the equine program at nearby Morrisville Agriculture and Technology College. Unfortunately, cancer shortened Larry's career. He was extremely popular among local horsemen and a big help to me in my early days with the horses.

My only win in a paramutual race was at Vernon Downs on May 28, 1992. I went to the front from the eight hole and won handily in 1:58:2. I won a race which was a terrific thrill. Soon after this race I retired from driving which made my wife very happy.

Misty's last year was in 1995 when he raced forty-two times (almost every week), won seven races, and took home $16,959. In 1997, the year I started sinking into a major depression period, *Misty* fell victim to arthritis and his great career was over. During eight years of racing he had two-hundred and fourteen starts, thirty-three wins, thirty seconds, twenty-four thirds, and earnings of $68,274.

JMF's Jamie's career was over after only four years of racing in Canada. His lifetime total was fifty-three starts, twelve wins, five seconds, five thirds, and earnings of $45,293.

Both *Jamie* and *Misty* had exactly the same lifetime record of 155:2. Of all standardbreds, only one out of every five horses makes the races and makes money. Only one out of every ten actually earns a profit for their owners. The fact that both *Misty* and *Jamie* succeeded, the first two horses born on the farm, was definitely beginners luck!

The Denny Brainard Memorial Trophy Race
July 23, 1999   JMF'S R D HALL   7th Race
Driver: Ron Hill Jr   2nd Armbro Nocturne
Owner: Peter Marshall   1:57   Tr: Peter Marshall

JMF'S SAM

September 28, 2002
One Mile PACE

Driver: Bill Bailey
Owner/Trainer:
Peter Marshall

Race: 1 #4
Time: 1:56

JMF's Sam—JMF's RD Hall

After the initial good luck with *Misty* and *Jamie*, reality set in and only two out of more than a dozen foals born later at the farm would be successful (before depression forced me out of the breeding business in 1997). They are *JMF's Sam* and *JMF's RD Hall.*

JMF's Sam was born on April 8, 1992, and I assisted the delivery that beautiful spring day. He reminded me immediately of his grandsire *National Star* and he entertained our family and scores of other fans here in Central New York for the last ten years. Standardbreds are required to retire when they turn fifteen years of age. At the farm, *Sam* is referred to as the *Iron Horse.* This is because he has held up so well and so long. Presently he is twelve years old and racing just as fast as ever. I'm confident that he will race until the age of fifteen when he is forced to retire.

Sam's entry into racing raised some eyebrows at the Syracuse Mile as a two-year-old when he beat some well-bred horses, winning in 157:0. Ron Hill was the driver that day and did a great job developing *Sam* in his early years. *Sam* is not the easiest horse to drive, but a pleasure to drive if you let him have his way. If you take him to the starting gate too early, causing the gate to slow him up, he will go nuts. Likewise, if the driver lets him get boxed in behind a tired horse he also will get mad and break stride. As I mentioned earlier, he inherited that great desire from his grandsire *National Star.*

Just before sending this book to be published, *Sam* won the feature race at Vernon Downs in 1:53:2. This was his lifetime best time at eleven years old, which is most remarkable. He was a long shot in the race with his odds going off at sixty-four to one. In the end he paid one hundred twenty-nine dollars and fifty cents for a two dollar win ticket. Unfortunately, Ruth and I were in Maine and missed the race.

At June 14, 2003, *Sam's* statistics show two-hundred and ninety-five starts, forty-five wins, forty-eight seconds, forty thirds, and earnings of $124,654. If only I had a barnful of horses like *Sam!*

JMF's RD Hall was born on April 25, 1993, and was named after my good friend and accountant Bob Hall. Bob informed me that he had several clients that owned horses over the years and all of them lost money. I replied that I would be the first to make money, and to prove it I would name a horse after him. I wouldn't say that I have made money on horses, but have come pretty close to breaking even, which in the horse business is fantastic. My prediction that *JMF's RD Hall* would be a winner has come true. *RD* is a trotter and *Sam* is a pacer. For these that don't know the difference, trotting is a natural gait of the horse where the front foot leaves the ground a split second before the rear foot comes down.

Pacing is different. Both the front and rear legs on the same side move forward and back in unison. This is an unnatural gait for the horse and, almost always, hobbles are added to the legs to insure that the horse stays on pace.

Trotting is a much more precise coordination and breaking stride is much more of a problem with trotters than with pacers. Also, pacers tend to be faster than trotters.

There is an interesting story about the breeding of *Countess Lyrical* that resulted in the birth of *JMF's RD Hall*.

Countess Lyrical had decent breeding, but was on the way to the slaughter house when I bought her for four-hundred dollars. The first breeding was to *Hamilton White* and this produced a colt I named *JMF's Peter* after my son Peter. *JMF's Peter* did make the races but was a real nut and I sold him. In his five-year career he had ninety-four starts, three wins, eight seconds, twelve thirds, and earnings of $10,727. You would not like to pay a training bill of a thousand dollars a month and have a horse like *Peter*.

In the spring of 1989 I decided to breed *Countess Lyrical* to the stallion *Came to Pass* that was standing at nearby Morrisville College. In standardbreds, artificial breeding is used almost exclusively. This is not allowed in the thoroughbreds where natural cover is required. When *Countess Lyrical* was ready to breed, I traveled to Morrisville and picked up the collected semen and returned to the farm to inseminate the mare. At Morrisville, the sample was placed in a plastic vial with a sealed lid. The vial was then wrapped in a large roll of cotton to keep it from becoming chilled during the 15 minute ride back to the farm.

When I arrived at the farm and removed the cotton that was insulating the vial, I found that the top lid had popped off the vial in the transit. The vial was empty. All of the semen had soaked into the cotton. Since another sample could not be obtained for two more days, I wrung out the cotton like a dish rag, collected a few cc's of the semen, and inseminated the mare. She conceived!

RD proved to be a problem from the start and continues to be a problem to this day. He would refuse to turn going to the gate, run off the track, and break stride frequently. However, he did have that all important ability—speed! Once again, Ron Hill was helpful in working with *RD*, adding trotting hobbles to his harness and enduring his lousy attitude.

In 2001 *RD's* problems were exhausting my patience. He made only ten starts that year and only made $2,010. I entered him in a horse auction at the Meadowlands and was eager to say goodbye. My son Peter pleaded with me to keep him.

Finally I agreed to cancel the sale and gave him to Peter. Now Peter would have to put up with his antics. Under Peter's care *RD* dramatically improved, making $20,933 in 2002 and has done well so far in 2003.

As of June 16, 2003, *RD's* career totals are one-hundred and ninety-seven starts, forty-two wins, twenty-seven seconds, twenty-five thirds, and earnings of $125,134. I should have named more horses after my accountant!

In December of 2001, I started looking for stallions to breed two trotting mares that I had acquired. The recovery from depression in 2000 had restored my energy and I wanted to get back to seeing some newborn foals at the farm every spring.

When I called Morrisville about *Came to Pass* I was told that they had retired him as a stallion and was leased to a thoroughbred farm in Maryland where he was used as a teaser. Following a discussion with Dave Hansen, my friend at Morrisville, I was able to lease the stallion. I found a way to get him shipped back up to the farm and also get him registered as a New York State qualified stallion.

JMF's RD Hall's sire, *Came to Pass* is now at the farm. At this moment he has sired two fillys, *JMF's Peg* that was born on April 6, 2003, and *JMF's Laura* that was born on March 13, 2004. One mare is presently pregnant to *Came to Pass,* and will hopefully foal soon. Hopefully his offspring will succeed, and once again create an interest in his future reproductive career.

You Know What I Mean—I Know What You Mean

Both of these horses, with these unusual names were winners. The USTA (United States Trotting Association) is the governing force of harness racing. No two horses can have the same name, and the total number of letters and space in a proposed name cannot exceed eighteen. Therefore, in the program you will see a variety of unusual and often comical names that the owners have come up with. Once a horse races in an official race, the name can never be changed. Before they race for a modest fee of twenty-eight dollars, you can change the name to anything you want, as long as the name is not on record of being used for another horse. I have done this several times.

For simplification I'll refer to these two horses as *You Know* and *I Know*, just like we did at the farm.

You Know was purchased at a New York auction in January of 1988. He had spectacular breeding. *Abercrombie*, a very famous stallion, was his sire and *Armbro Concerto* by *Most Happy Fella* was his dam. At the sale I had crossed him off as too expensive for me. When the bidding slowed up at twenty-five hundred dollars, I suddenly became very interested. He appeared to be sound with no obvious problems, so I entered the bidding and bought him for thirty-two hundred dollars. I thought that this was a bargain since the stud fee for *Abercrombie* at that time was twenty-five grand, and someone had already cared for him for three years. The dam had already sired some outstanding individuals. The potential to succeed was definitely there.

When I trucked *You Know* back to the farm, I soon found out why he hadn't raced as a two-year-old and why no one wanted to buy him at the sale. He had a huge attitude problem. He would not even walk fast and the more you whipped him, he would come to a complete stop. I suddenly wished I had my thirty-two hundred back in the bank instead of this horse.

He obviously had been abused and this caused his bad attitude. Karl Lowes, a gifted Canadian horseman was at the farm that year and gave *You Know* plenty of TLC and patience. It paid off! His inherited potential started to come out. In his first race at Vernon Downs he won, upsetting the odds-on favorite. The favorite was ahead of all his competitors by ten lengths at the head of the stretch. The owners and several guests (dressed to the nines) were headed to the winners circle for their picture and victory celebration.

Suddenly from last place, *You Know* made a tremendous run for the wire, caught up with the favorite, and pushed his nose ahead right at the finish. The large party trudged back to their tables, obviously disappointed. Who was this unknown horse *You Know What I Mean*??

You Know had made his classic debut and would delight fans for the next several years with his late rush for the finish line. He would almost always be dead last at the three-quarter pole and would take off on the outside and pass several horses, almost all of them, winning by just enough. He always knew exactly where the finish line was and came to a stop soon after.

A broken bone in his foot (coffin bone) sidelined his great career. He did recover to race after the fracture, but was never the same. *You Know What I Mean* was a great horse and one of my favorites. He entertained a lot of race fans for nine years. His career featured two-hundred and fifty-two starts, thirty wins, thirty-nine seconds, forty-seven thirds, and earnings of $90,612. Ironically, his fastest win was 1:55:2, exactly the same as *Jamie* and *Misty*. Owning this horse was great therapy for my depression—you know what I mean?

I Know What You Mean was purchased as a yearling in New York at the Meadowlands sale in 1990. At the sale I was looking for only those horses that were eligible for the New York State Sire Stakes. The Sire Stakes is a lucrative opportunity to make big money if you are lucky enough to own an outstanding horse (two-year-old or three-year-old) that is eligible. To be eligible the sire must be standing (in residence) in New York State at the time of conception. Everyone owning an eligible offspring of these stallions contributes about nine hundred dollars. In New York State every year, over seven million dollars is distributed to the many winners of specified races held all across New York State at different tracks. An outstanding performer can easily win two hundred to three hundred thousand dollars if he or she goes undefeated. Every owner's dream is to own one of these fortunate horses. They arrive once in a lifetime and often not ever.

At the sale, I ran into a fellow Veterinarian, with his owner, who was also interested in New York State eligible horses. I found out what horses he was interested in and we agreed not to bid against each other. My absolute top limit was five thousand dollars. Most of the horses sold much higher. At the time, I had no idea who the owner, who Dr. Keller had with him, was. He obviously had some financial clout and ended up buying some expensive yearlings. Later, I would learn that this individual was Patrick Bennet, who presently is in jail for masterminding the largest financial Ponzi scheme in U.S. history.

Finally, a nice looking filly entered the ring that Keller and Bennet were not interested in. Her sire was *Niatross*, who at that time was the fastest horse in the world. I was sure she would be too expensive, but my final bid of five thousand dollars (my absolute limit) bought the filly.

I can't remember her name, but when she arrived at the farm Brian Carson suggested a better name. He said, "Doc, you should name this filly *I Know What You Mean*," and I did.

I Know proved to have a wonderful flowing gait and very fast. My inexperience at that time led me to train her too hard and she had problems staying sound. If I did things differently, I know she could have easily won two-hundred thousand in her two-and-three-year-old races. A great horse needs to find a great trainer and at that time I made some mistakes.

Female horses (mares and fillies), like two-legged females, can be very temperamental. You have to train their attitude (their mind) more than their body. This will be explained in more detail later when I tell you about *Sister Gold*. Despite the many mistakes I made, *I Know* did have a successful career. In 1995, I decided to try to breed *I Know* to *Black Gold Road* who had arrived at the farm. She did not get pregnant, so I decided to race her again in claimers at Vernon Downs. One day between races, I was breeding another mare (artificially) and decided to split the semen sample and inseminate *I Know* one more time. The next weekend the same horseman at Vernon that also claimed another great horse of mine previously (*Call My Lawyer*) claimed *I Know*.

Claiming horses is legalized kidnapping. When you enter a horse in a claiming race, the owner accepts the risk of losing the horse at the moment that particular race starts. There is an unwritten honor code between owners and trainers that know each other that you don't claim horses from fellow trainers. Often horses are put in claiming races because they cannot compete in condition races. The training bill on a given horse is the income that supports this trainer's family. The claiming price definitely puts a price tag on the horse.

Sometimes the owner and trainer are agreeable to sell the horse for the claiming price privately. However, reputable trainers and owners do not kidnap horses from fellow horsemen that they know. If someone comes in from out of the area and takes your horse you have to accept it. I have never questioned a claim from someone I did not know.

This individual that I had previously befriended at my farm (that claimed two horses that I liked) will never recover my respect. I will never recognize him as a fellow human being for the rest of my days.

I have only claimed one horse in my life and that was a horse that had been claimed from me previously. I rekidnapped one of my children back. This will be explained when I talk about *Sister Gold*.

The new owner of *I Know What You Mean* continued to race this nice mare and spent the next winter in Florida pushing her for all he could get from her.

She did win a couple of races and he finally sold her to a Canadian horseman when her racing ability faded.

Early in 1996, she raced three times and did not make a dime. This great horseman could not understand her poor performance. She was heavily pregnant! Apparently she conceived from my last breeding at the farm.

He had beat on this pregnant mare, racing all winter. How could he possibly not recognize and respect her condition?

Following her sale, she arrived at a Canadian farm and was turned out in a pasture. A few days later, the new owner was surprised to find out he had purchased two horses instead of one! She had foaled overnight. I felt so sad that I couldn't care for her at the farm during her pregnancy. This is a clear example of cruelty to animals. Someday I hope I can find out what happened to her foal. I have located her recently in Canada and hope to buy her back as a broodmare on my farm in the future.

Unfortunately, *I Know* never realized her potential. Her career ended on this sad note, but she still had accomplished one-hundred and one starts, fourteen wins, two seconds, twelve thirds, and earnings of $24,379.

Call My Lawyer

In January of 1994, I traveled back down to the Meadowlands horse sale. My hope was to find a classy horse that I could rehabilitate at the farm. The year before I had constructed an indoor swimming facility and had started swimming horses as a training exercise. We had been swimming horses in an outside pond for several years, but when winter arrives this option terminates.

Most successful horse trainers move their stables south for the winter, but I wanted no part of this nomadic life. A few indoor swimming facilities existed and I checked them out. Most of them were way too expensive for me to duplicate. I finally developed my own idea of constructing one I could afford.

There was only one spot on the farm that I wanted the pool located. When the large backhoe dug down to the bottom of the pit for the pool, we found quicksand. Walking over the surface that would be the foundation of the pool was like walking on a bowl of Jell-O. Tommy Sears was running the backhoe. I held a sixteen foot two-by-six board on end and asked Tom to punch the two-by-six down into the quicksand to find the solid bottom. The sixteen foot two-by-six went down like a toothpick in a cake!

I was distraught! There isn't a contractor in the world that would go ahead with the construction over this area of quicksand. However, this is where I wanted the pool—so I went ahead with my idea. We put twelve inches of number two crushed stone over the quicksand and then poured the pool with six thousand dollars worth of cement.

Every night for the next several months I would toss and turn wondering what would happen. The pool did tilt one inch to the east but then stopped. It has not moved anymore in the last ten years, so I don't worry about it sinking out of sight when I go to bed anymore.

Once the eighteen-foot-square cement base was in, we built a ramp for the horses to enter and exit the pool. Finally, I had a pole barn built over the pool with six drying stalls. We had a year-round swimming facility for swimming and rehabilitating horses.

Since we could not train our horses not to poop while swimming, keeping the water clean was a problem. We swim eight to twelve horses every day in the pool and most of them like to poop in the pool. Picking the *road apples* off the surface with a screen helps, but brown water develops quickly. Filtration equipment was impossible on my budget. Our solution is to completely drain the pool every three months, clean the poop that settles to the bottom, and refill the pool from a nearby spring fed pond.

The water is not heated but the building is. I am able to heat the thirty-six by forty-eight well-insulated building for less than five dollars a day during our bitter cold winters. The drying stalls have heat lamps and fans that quickly dry the horses.

Once the horses get used to entering the pool, they seem to enjoy the swim and go in readily. (Just like kids on the Fourth of July.) We hold the horses in place with a tail tie secured to steel posts along the pool perimeter. The hair on a horse's tail is extremely strong and holding the horses in place with this method is very effective and not painful to the horse. They totally enjoy it and most of our older horses at the farm swim five to ten minutes every day and only see a harness at the race track every weekend at the races.

Since today's race tracks are stone dust (very hard), the swimming creates cardio-vascular exertion with no stress on their legs and feet. The trainers enjoy the ease of this conditioning. We sit by the pool chatting and drinking coffee while the horses are swimming. The pool can accommodate two horses swimming at the same time.

We do chlorinate the water to kill all bacteria. One extremely beneficial result from swimming I found out by accident. Just before a horse enters the pool we add about two quarts of liquid chlorine. As the swimming churns the water the chlorine gas works out of the water. The horses, while swimming, breathe very hard and inhale this chlorine gas for this five to ten minute period.

I have concluded over the years that this respiratory therapy is the greatest benefit to the horse in our swimming program. Oxygen passes from the air to the blood only at the very depths of the lung in small sacs called alveoli. The chlorine gas seems to remove mucous and bacteria that often block these areas of lung tissue. The horse that can get the most oxygen at the end of the race is more likely to realize their maximum ability. All our swimming horses finish their races strong!

So with this *ace in the hole* advantage back at the farm, I carefully looked over the horses at the annual 1994 sale at the Meadowlands track in New Jersey.

Soon, I spied a beautiful, classy six-year-old horse named *Call My Lawyer*. He was obviously in a lot of pain and could not bear weight on one of his hind legs. This horse had been an open pacer at the Meadowlands and had made his previous owner over one-hundred and fifty thousand dollars. Can you imagine dumping a wonderful horse in a sale to get rid of him after making all that money, plus over twenty trips to the winners circle??

If he didn't have the bad leg, he would have sold for seventy to eighty thousand dollars, but no one wanted a lame horse, so I bought him for three thousand dollars. This was my first major challenge for my rehabilitation program back at the farm.

We called him *Lawyer* at the farm and I fell in love with him immediately. First I took him to the Cornell Veterinary Equine Clinic in Ithaca, New York, for x-rays and minor surgery to remove bone chips in one hock joint. This cost me seventeen hundred dollars, which I considered a good investment. Back at the farm he healed quickly and enjoyed his daily workouts in the pool. In six months he was all healed up and I raced him once at Vernon Downs as a tightener.

A few days later, Ruth and I left for Maine for a short vacation. I wanted to race him at the Syracuse Mile (the State Fairgrounds one-mile track), which is near our farm. The only race he qualified for was a twelve-thousand-dollar claimer. I told my son Peter to enter him in this race and give me a call afterwards with the results.

When Peter called me in Maine that *Lawyer* had been claimed by the same horse trainer that would later also claim my mare *I Know What You Mean*. I was shocked and distraught. It was just like receiving the news that one of my children had been kidnapped. I knew this horseman could not come up with twelve thousand dollars on the best day of his life. Soon I found out that he had convinced his father-in-law to lend him the money. This man was a successful, retired engineer, and a good friend. I had got to know him when his son-in-law stabled horses at my farm. I saw him a few days later at the track and told him what I thought of him. His wife, if still alive, would never have let him claim my horse. He was a man of character and I believe he deeply regretted this betrayal of our friendship. He died less than a year later (a broken man) and I did not attend his wake.

This horseman pushed *Lawyer* to the limit and broke him down again in a few months. I never could watch him race after he was kidnapped from me. Soon he was back on the garbage heap of horses. This great horse ended up either in the slaughter house or pulling a buggy for the Amish.

If I could have kept him on my swim program he would have entertained us every Saturday night (until retirement at age fifteen) and then a nice pasture retirement. I will always regret putting this great horse in that one claiming race.

Racing seven years, *Lawyer* had one-hundred and forty-eight starts, twenty-eight wins, eighteen seconds, nineteen thirds, and earnings of $172,391. His lifetime record of 1:51:4 qualified him as the fastest horse to ever set four feet on my farm.

Black Gold Road

BGR was born to very famous parents. His sire was *On The Road Again*, the leading sire in New York State, and his dam was *Albaquel*, a daughter of *Albatross*, whose offspring had earnings of over one million dollars.

BGR was trained by Doug Ackerman, one of the leading trainers in America. He showed promise as a two-year-old, racing twenty-one times and making $69,143. His three-year-old season was sensational, racing nineteen times with six wins, one second, four thirds, and earnings of $136,448. In the 1991 *Little Brown Jug*, the top race for three-year-old pacers in the country, he placed fourth in an elimination race and missed the final. The three horses ahead of him at the wire were: *Precious Bunny*, *Die Laughing*, and *Three Wizzards*, all leading sires in the country today.

Problems staying sound troubled his career for the next three years, making only fourteen starts in 1992, 1993, and 1994 combined. I found him by accident while visiting a farm near Goshen, New York. He had bred a few mares the year before but the owner had been told that he could never race again.

I probably could have bought him outright for about two grand. Instead, I convinced the owner that I would try my swimming program on him. If he did make it to the races, we would split the earnings fifty-fifty and I would get free breeding to my mares. He agreed to this lease arrangement.

BGR loved the swimming and turnout program. His mind and body improved and I felt confident that he could race again. And race again he did! In 1995 he made thirty-three starts, seven wins, four seconds, seven thirds, and earnings of $29,310. Now I regretted the lease agreement since half his earnings would go to the owner. Finally, I purchased *BGR* for twelve thousand dollars and terminated the lease. Although this was ten thousand more than I could have bought him for originally, it was still a wise financial deal for me. If I would have waited till the end of the year, he would have been paid fifteen grand and still owned the horse.

One of his biggest wins that year was the day of my daughter Jennifer's wedding. After paying the bill for the nice reception at the Calvary Club, I learned that *BGR* had won just enough money to pay for the reception. I was elated, but found out the next morning playing golf that it wasn't quite enough. The bartender ran out on the course and told me he forgot the vodka. I owed him another three hundred bucks.

This great year with *BGR* convinced a few people that swimming programs can be successful. Besides winning almost thirty thousand dollars, *BGR* lowered his record time for a win by almost three seconds to 1:53:4.

The next year his racing career was over. Even swimming could not help his many problems and he was retired to stud.

I convinced a friend to purchase two of his offspring that were born the year prior to my acquisition. They were two fillies: *Sister Gold* and *So Sharp*. This owner decided he didn't want to pay a training bill so I bought the two horses from him. They both made the races. *So Sharp* was very mediocre and was sold after two years of racing. *Sister Gold* was definitely a fast horse, but also had a very bad attitude problem. I'll tell you about her later.

In 1997, depression destroyed my energy and enthusiasm for the farm. *BGR* was sold to a friend who needed a stallion.

BGR had a career of one-hundred and four starts, twenty-one wins, twelve seconds, seventeen thirds, and earnings of $257,519. *BGR* was truly a great horse.

Syracuse Post Standard 1-22-03

DR. JAMES MARSHALL, a veterinarian, takes his horse Sister Gold for a swim Tuesday at his farm in North Chittenango.

Sister Gold's Silver Lining

Horse reclaims her winning ways after midlife stumbles

By Debra J. Groom
Staff writer

At one time, Sister Gold was about to end up in the proverbial trash heap of horses.

At about age 5, after a number of years winning harness races, she developed a bad attitude. She was prone to stop in the middle of a race and start going backward.

She didn't want to race. She was a mere whisker away from ending up working on an Amish farm.

Then her owner, Dr. James Marshall, of Manlius, diagnosed the bay mare as having an early midlife crisis and got her back on firm footing at his farm in North Chittenango. He nursed her, rehabilitated her and trained her.

In 2002, Sister Gold had more harness racing wins than any other pacer or trotter in the United States, according to statistics kept by the U.S. Trotting Association. Racing at the Saratoga harness track, the mare had 25 first places, nine seconds and three thirds in 46 starts.

"This just shows how durable this horse is. That's an extraordinary amount of races," said John Pawlak of the trotting association.

"Horses like those in the Kentucky Derby are likely to start 10 times," he said. "This horse had 46 tries. It's quite a feather in the cap of the owner and trainer."

While Marshall and his son, Peter, are well-known in the area for training race horses, they are just part of the Sister Gold success story.

Marshall owned the mare from the time she was a yearling, when he bought her and her sister, So Sharp, about 1995.

"She started racing at Vernon Downs

Sister Gold's record

1996: 20 starts, five wins, earned $13,687
1997: 34 starts, four wins, earned $15,060
1998: 37 starts, six wins, earned $7,387
1999: 33 starts, four wins, earned $8,952
2000: 15 starts, no wins, earned $1,491
2001: 17 starts, no wins, earned $2,462
2002: 46 starts, 25 wins, earned $29,688

Source: U.S. Trotting Association

and was pretty successful," Marshall said. "We trained her and she won up to $50,000 as a 2-year-old, 3-year-old and 4-year-old."

Then the horse started to go through something similar to menopause.

"It has something to do with her female hormones. She was temperamental and had a bad attitude," Marshall said. "And in 2001 it really got bad. She wouldn't race. I couldn't get a driver to drive her."

He tried to sell her to an Amish farmer. But the farmer thought she had a contagious disease because he felt a swelling under her jaw.

She wasn't sick, Marshall said, but the farmer "wouldn't take her." So Marshall put Sister Gold on a hormone called Regumate, which is used often on mares with behavioral problems.

"She didn't win one race in 2001," Marshall said. "But her attitude did start to improve in the fall of 2001."

Marshall started rehabbing the horse, putting her through her paces on a small track and swimming in his horse pool.

"She got more interested in racing,"

he said.

But since Sister Gold had such a horrible reputation at Vernon Downs — the stopping and going backward hijinks didn't endear her to track drivers — Marshall started racing her in claiming races in Saratoga.

Claiming races help level the playing field of competition in races and help boost the amount of the purse available in the race, said John Leonard of Saratoga Equine Sports Center.

But, while the horse owners get more money if their horses win, place or show, they also risk losing the animals because anyone, if he or she has the cash, can buy the horse with no questions asked.

This is what happened to Sister Gold.

She won four in a row in $2,500 claiming races. She won again in a $4,000 claiming race. Then she didn't do well in a $6,000 claiming race.

In the next $4,000 claiming race, she won but was claimed by Gary Leonardi, of Saratoga. Leonardi claimed Sister Gold on April 14 and trained her through 31 of her 46 starts last year.

With Leonardi as owner and trainer, Sister Gold won 19 firsts, four seconds and two thirds at Saratoga. With the Marshalls, she had 15 starts, winning six times, placing second five times and coming in third once.

"On Dec. 27, in a $3,000 claimer, I reclaimed her and brought her home," Marshall said. "She has sentimental value."

Right now, Sister Gold is enjoying a bit of a vacation, but come spring, she will be back on the track. Marshall says he hopes to race her 25 to 30 times in 2003 on half-mile tracks like Saratoga and Batavia.

Sister Gold

Sister Gold needed a full-time psychiatrist instead of a veterinarian to handle her development.

She did have speed and was flawlessly gaited. I can't even remember her making a break in the eight years I raced her. However, she was a supreme test for my patience more than once.

As a two-and-three-year-old she made nearly thirty thousand dollars, and stayed sound. Peter and I had a lot of fun racing her at several county fairs during her first two years. At one fair race she had a temper tantrum as the race started and threw herself on the ground. All the other horses left the starting point and were thirty lengths ahead of her when she finally got back on her feet and decided she wanted to try to race. Everyone watching the race was totally amazed. She caught up to the other horses and won the race.

Her four-and-five-year-old seasons were so-so, winning $7,387 in 1998 and $8,952 in 1999. Then in 2000 and 2001 her attitude became a serious problem. She just didn't want to race anymore. Over that two-year period she did not win a race. Sometimes she would stop in the middle of the race track and start to back up. The more the driver would whip her, the worse she would get. Her reputation at Vernon Downs was terrible. No one would drive her in a race.

I decided to sell her in August of 2001 and told an Amish horse dealer to stop by the farm. He offered me eleven hundred dollars for the mare which I accepted. Good riddance to bad rubbish. When this man started to load *Sister Gold* onto his trailer he noticed a swelling under her jaw and suspected she was coming down with strangles. This is a very contagious strep infection in horses that everyone wants to avoid. He negated the sale. I knew she didn't have strangles, but I was stuck with her.

At the time, Sherry Hunt, her caretaker, loved her and begged me to give her another chance. Since I had no other choice I started giving her Regumate, an expensive hormone that blocks the estrogen which is normally secreted from the ovaries.

Her attitude improved and I just swam her every day. Once a week I put the harness on and trained her. She actually had a turnaround and wanted to race. I never carried a whip.

The problem at Vernon was that no one would drive her. Finally one driver agreed to drive her but kept behind all of the horses in case she stopped. This method was safe for the driver but gave her no chance to win the race.

Early in 2002 I took her to Saratoga Harness where they race all winter. Here the drivers did not know about her bad reputation. I instructed Brian Walker, a driver at Saratoga, to take her right to the front as soon as the starting gate left. She had tremendous gate speed and could reach the front from any post position. She won her first race, the first race she had won in over two years. I entered her in the cheapest claiming race which was twenty-five hundred dollars. She won four races in a row! Afraid that she might be claimed, I entered her next in a four-thousand-dollar claimer. She won again. People were showing an interest in her ability so I raised her to a six-thousand-dollar claimer, which was too much for her. The following week I dropped her back down to the four-thousand-dollar claimer. She won again and the leading trainer at Saratoga claimed her. In six weeks I had won over seven thousand dollars, winning six of seven races, and had the claiming check of forty-eight hundred. (Mares get a twenty-five percent allowance.) This was not a bad result for a mare that I tried to sell for eleven hundred dollars just four months earlier.

The new owner found out about the secret hormone treatment I used on *Sister Gold*. She continued to race superbly at Saratoga and went on to win nineteen more races.

The last race of the year the owner dropped her down to a three-thousand-dollar claimer and I went up and claimed her back. This was the only time I ever claimed a horse. I brought her home to the swimming pool and a rest.

Despite no wins in 2000 and 2001, she won twenty-five races in 2002 which is the most races any horse in North America won that year. She was written up in the local paper with her whole story: "*Sister Gold* has a silver lining!"

After a short rest I took her back to Saratoga and raced her in five-thousand-dollar claimers, which were a little too much for her. On February fourteenth another Valentine's Day massacre occurred: the same trainer claimed her back from me for another check for forty-eight hundred dollars. She was pretty much pooped out and hasn't raced in seven months. Her bad attitude returned. I will not claim her back. She was very good to me financially, but her lousy attitude kept me from loving her.

As of June 16, 2003, *Sister Gold* had made two-hundred and seven starts, forty-four wins, thirty-four seconds, twenty-six thirds, and earnings of $79,097.

Stage Door Stevie

Probably the most famous horse to ever reside at our farm was *Stage Door Stevie*. *Stevie* was owned by a Veterinarian friend of mine, George Halpern, who practiced in nearby Baldwinsville.

In 1986 *Stage Door Stevie* was rated the number-one two-year-old pacing colt in the country. During his freshman year he raced thirteen times and won every race, earning $87,897. The following year he raced twenty-one times, winning thirteen races, second twice, third once, and earnings of $260,223.

A serious knee injury sidelined *Stevie* in 1990. He had only nine starts, two wins, one second, three thirds, and earnings of $7,884. He would limp badly before and after each race, but he had a tremendous heart and would block out his pain during the race. Finally all the drivers feared that he would go down in a race and refused to drive him.

In 1991, I ran into George Halpern at the track and we chatted about *Stevie*. I asked him if we could try a swimming program. He was planning to put *Stevie* down but agreed to give the horse to my son Peter. We brought *Stevie* to the farm and started swimming him every day. I agreed that I would put *Stevie* down and bury him at the farm if rehabilitation failed.

After several months, his pain disappeared and I thought he could race again. All the drivers at Vernon were skeptical and refused to drive him. He was branded as a cripple and every driver fears driving a horse that might go down in a race. No one can be critical of this fear because the risk of injury is very great if this happens.

At that time, Don Cole, a wealthy owner of the Cole Muffler chain in New York State, built a race track at Alexandria Bay near the popular Thousand Islands vacation area in Northern New York. He called the track *Bonnie Castle Downs* after a popular resort that he also owned in the area.

In August of 1991, a series of races was held at that track. There was a race for *Stevie* and Peter and I agreed to enter the great horse in this race. No one would drive him so I decided to drive him myself. The race was two heats of one mile each. The track was half a mile in length, requiring two trips around to complete the mile. Peter and I agreed that if he sored up after the first race we would scratch out of the second race.

Stevie was clearly the greatest horse I have ever driven. They had a small grandstand that was packed, plus a local announcer who was obviously enjoying his assignment. When *Stevie* came onto the track and saw all the noisy fans his ears perked up and he was really enjoying the opportunity to race again.

When the starting gate left, *Stevie* rocketed to the front and showed off his ability. Soon, I could not see or hear any horses behind us. He won the race by thirty lengths.

When I turned to jog back past the grandstand, everyone was on their feet clapping and voicing their approval of *Stevie's* performance. The local announcer was screaming over the sound system: "*Stage Door Stevie* with Dr. Marshall driving just broke the track record here at *Bonnie Castle Downs* in 2:04:4." Both the horse and driver were pleased with all of this recognition.

After the race, Peter and I checked *Stevie's* bad knee. He still seemed free of pain so we decided to also race in the second heat after a forty-five minute rest.

The second race was a carbon copy of the first. *Stevie* won the race by even a greater margin. When we jogged back by the grandstand the fans were clapping and yelling even louder. The local announcer was screaming over the loudspeaker: "*Stage Door Stevie* and Dr. Marshall have just re-broke the track record in 2:04:2!"

This was definitely the highlight of my driving career. In reality, any driver in the world would have accomplished the same results. *Stevie* was just a great horse. Later I would win a race driving *JMF's Misty* at Vernon Downs. This was a thrill but the two wins with *Stage Door Stevie* at *Bonnie Castle Downs* were the pinnacle of my driving career. I was fifty-eight years old when I received my drivers "P" license. I had some close calls driving at fairs and finally promised my wife that I wouldn't drive again.

Following those two races the inflammation in *Stevie's* knee returned. About a month later we were taking other horses to a county fair at Whitney Point and decided to take *Stevie* along also. About halfway on the first trip around the fair track I heard a snap indicating a broken bone and stopped *Stevie* immediately.

Back at the farm, we could not remedy the constant pain. After conferring with Dr. Halpern the decision was to terminate his suffering. He is buried along the main entrance to the farm. In my opinion, *Stevie* is still the greatest horse ever to touch my life and the farm.

His career totals were seventy-two starts, thirty-seven wins, eight seconds, six thirds, and earnings of $386,471.

Apache but standard 4/24/03

Michelle Gabel / Staff photographer

RETIRED VETERINARIAN James Marshall (*left*) and Margherita Martinez, an employee of the James Marshall farm in North Chittenango, check out Baltic Mist and her foal, JMF's Peg, on Thursday. Baltic Mist, a 12-year-old Standardbred, had an intra-abdominal abscess and underwent surgery while she was pregnant.

Racehorse Mom Beats Odds

Mare carries foal to term despite serious illness, treatment

By Debra J. Groom
Staff writer

A sure sign of spring is new babies in the barnyard.

But the new addition at the James Marshall farm in North Chittenango is not only a sign of spring, but also a bit of an Easter season miracle.

The April 6 birth of filly JMF's Peg is remarkable because her mother, Baltic Mist, was discovered to have a serious illness while she was pregnant.

Fayetteville resident Marshall, a retired veterinarian who now rehabilitates racehorses, said the 12-year-old Standardbred had an intra-abdominal abscess and underwent surgery in late August to remove the mass.

Vets were concerned about the surgery, thinking it could cause the mare to abort.

"She was critical, so they had to do the surgery in the middle of the night," Marshall said of the vets at the Cornell University Hospital for Animals in Ithaca.

"It is kind of a miracle that she made it. But they thought she most likely would lose it (the foal)," he said.

Marshall said Baltic Mist first became ill in late June. She had lost weight during a 2-month period, but Marshall thought that was a result of her nursing a previous foal.

But, after the foal was weaned, Baltic Mist didn't get any better. It was thought she had colic, a collection of gas in the intestines that causes extreme pain.

During exploratory surgery, the mass was found, Marshall said.

"It was a critical situation — the abscess was in the small intestine," Marshall said. "I tried to treat her, but there was no response.

"If she didn't have the surgery, she would die."

Dr. Brett Woodie, a large breed veterinary surgeon at Cornell University who performed the surgery, said Baltic Mist "was a sick horse."

She not only had the large abscess on the small intestine, but quite a bit of the intestine was "twisted and had numerous kinks in it."

He said the abscess and 10 to 12 feet of small intestine was removed. A horse has 70 to 75 feet of small intestine.

Woodie was concerned about the pregnancy because Baltic Mist was very sick and had to endure the stress of surgery and anesthesia.

"We felt if she maintained the preg-

nancy postoperatively, we thought she would carry to term," Woodie said.

Marshall said Baltic Mist came out of the surgery well, and the pregnancy continued. But she then had to take a number of antibiotics and other drugs, and there still was a concern for the foal.

"If it was born with birth defects, I would have to put it to sleep," Marshall said. "I didn't want that as an ending to this saga."

On April 6 — two weeks before Easter — Baltic Mist delivered normally. JMF's Peg already is prancing around the paddock and soon will take to the pasture so people driving down New Boston Road will be able to see her.

Woodie said the removal of intestine does not affect Baltic Mist's life and also will not keep her from bearing more foals.

"She's a super nice horse," the vet said.

He added, "We're delighted" with her progress and the foal.

Marshall is hoping JMF's Peg will be a good racehorse like her mom and dad. Came to Pass.

"The vet bill for Baltic Mist was $6,000. I need to justify this expense," he laughed.

Came to Pass—Baltic Mist

We all hope that our children are successful in life. Likewise, every horseman's dream is to own both the stallion and the mare that produces a champion. Success on the race track pays the bills, but having successful offspring can be even more rewarding.

Both *Came to Pass* and *Baltic Mist* never succeeded as race-horses, but now that they both are mine, and residing at the farm, maybe their four-legged children will make it.

Came To Pass is a son of *Speedy Crown*, a very famous trotting stallion. At the time, *Came To Pass* was conceived, the stud fee for *Speedy Crown* was $25,000. He also had great blood on his maternal side. Earlier in this chapter I told you about him as the sire of *JMF's RD Hall.* He has a few other successful offspring, but in December of 2001 Morrisville decided to drop him from their stallion ranks. I found out that he had moved to Maryland where he was being used as a teaser on a Thoroughbred farm. A lease agreement was worked out with Dave Hansen at Morrisville and I sent two hundred dollars to register him as a stallion for the 2002 breeding season. This qualified any offspring for the lucrative Sire Stakes races in New York State during their two-year-old and three-year-old racing seasons. Over seven million dollars is distributed to the winners every year at five different tracks across New York State. In harness racing, the winner gets fifty percent of the purse, second gets twenty-five percent, third gets twelve percent, fourth gets eight percent, and fifth gets five percent. Recently, Dave Hansen decided that *Came To Pass's* ownership should be transferred to me. To make it legal I had to pay a dollar. This was one of the best buys of my life.

At the present time (March 2004), I have three trotting broodmares in foal to *Came To Pass*. The foals will arrive in April of 2004, and hopefully at least one of them will be a winner.

Baltic Mist is not a perfect specimen, but I like her blood lines. She is small and nearly blind in her right eye. I found her in an auction at Morrisville. She was called out of the ranks of the college's band of broodmares. At the time of the sale she was in foal to *Movie Mogul*, a decent trotting stallion. I felt a thousand dollars would buy her, but another bidder wouldn't give up. My final bid of twenty-six hundred dollars bought the mare—much more than she was worth.

The next spring she had a beautiful filly that I named *JMF's Sarah* after my beautiful granddaughter. Presently, *Sarah* is a three-year-old and showing some promise on the race track.

Baltic Mist was bred back to *Came To Pass*, who was still at Morrisville, and in April of 2002 she delivered another filly that I named *JMF's Sister Zoe* after my fantastic Irish twin. Several years ago another filly was named *JMF's Zoe V*. This filly suffered a twisted intestine and had to be destroyed at the Cornell Veterinary College. Hopefully *JMF's Sister Zoe*, now a two-year-old, will be a winner.

In the spring of 2002, *Came To Pass* was residing at our farm and *Baltic Mist* conceived on her foal heat. Mares normally ovulate about nine days after foaling and can become pregnant again after a nine-day vacation. Since horses take eleven months, we are able to see the foal a month earlier the next spring. Although the conception rate is usually only twenty-five percent on the foal heat, we do like earlier foals, and therefore try to breed sometimes on the foal heat.

About three months into her pregnancy, *Baltic Mist* developed colic. I knew she had an intestinal blockage and rushed her to the Cornell Veterinary College, which is one and a half hours from the farm. The vets at Cornell confirmed my suspicion. The only chance of saving her was surgery, which they announced would cost six thousand dollars, win or lose. The policy when I was in school of taking care of Alumni gratis had definitely changed. They also predicted the pregnancy would terminate as a result of the lengthy surgical procedure.

I had to give her a chance for life even though the six grand was for more than she was worth. The surgery took several hours into the night. The blockage required the removal of over twelve feet of intestine. I did not stay to watch, but received a call later that she had lived through the surgery. The next few days were critical. When she started eating and had her first bowel movement everyone was ecstatic. The anastomosis (surgical correction of the intestine) was successful. Even more remarkable than the surgery was that she did not abort her pregnancy. This was truly a remarkable piece of surgery and a great tribute to Dr. Brett Woodie and the entire staff at the Cornell Equine Hospital.

When I picked up the mare, I paid a thousand dollars, leaving the balance due of five thousand dollars. Since we were now on a fixed income, I explained that it would take a while for the rest. The nice gal at the desk replied, "No, problem Dr. Marshall, take as long as you'd like." What she didn't explain is that I would be charged eighteen percent on the unpaid balance. Two months earlier I attended my forty-fifth reunion at Cornell and donated five thousand dollars to the Veterinary College. I thought of writing to the dean explaining that the college was probably getting a better return on the five grand I owed than the five grand I gave them in June. However, I didn't do it. Although I have contributed each year to the Veterinary College for the past forty-five years, today's computers treat everyone the same. Even a Cornell Veterinary Professor Emeritus received the same consideration—absolutely no favors! The reason for this is the diminishing state support for the college.

One of the senior students, Erica Hutten, chose this case for her senior seminar presentation. An Ithaca ice storm prevented my attendance at her seminar, which was well received.

Although *Baltic Mist* had survived, there was a worry that surgical adhesives would cause future colic and more surgery. Fortunately, so far so good.

On April 6, 2003, *Baltic Mist* delivered yet another beautiful filly foal. The foal's markings were exactly the same as *JMF's RD Hall* who I had given to Peter. Therefore, I gave the foal to Peter and he named her *JMF's Peg* after his friend Peggy Bovaird.

Debbie Groom, a reporter for the Post-Standard, wrote a nice article about *Baltic Mist* and *JMF's Peg*. She told the whole story under the heading *Racehorse Mom Beats Odds*.

Presently both mother and daughter are doing fine. *Baltic Mist* is pregnant again to *Came To Pass*. We're hoping for a colt after her last three filly foals.

Every Sunday we bring them in the stable for everyone to pet on our *Walk & Talk* sessions.

Caspari and all the other losers

After reading about these horses, you are probably thinking about investing in a racehorse and making a ton of money.

Now I have to tell you about all the losers.

Over the years I named horses born on the farm after my wife (twice), all my children, my sisters, my sons-in-law, my daughters-in-law, and friends. As I mentioned earlier in the book, only two horses have made significant income. *JMF's Sam*, named after my son-in-law Sam Vulcano, and *JMF's RD Hall*, named after my accountant Bob Hall.

In 1993, my son and son-in-law, plus several of their golfing buddies decided to invest in a racehorse. They pooled a considerable amount of money and wanted to buy a horse that was ready to race. My previous purchases were usually horses with problems that few people at the auction would be interested in. Following this method, the purchase price was low, but I had to treat and board them for a lengthy period before they were able to race.

Paying the full shot for the care and training of a racehorse can be an expensive proposition. The lowest rate is twenty dollars per day, going up to as high as seventy-five dollars per day, depending on the trainer and the value of the horse. Most Thoroughbred trainers in New York get the highest rates. The daily feeding and training rate, plus the vet and Farrier bills add up fast. At Vernon Downs, which is considered one of the cheapest tracks to stable, you can expect to pay at least a thousand dollars a month to own a racehorse.

The idea of buying a horse that is all ready to race or claiming a racehorse makes sense. Using this method, your horse can race and win money to pay for all the bills, and hopefully make you a profit.

In January of 1993 with the help of an experienced horseman, I attended a New York auction of racehorses. The horseman picked out the perfect horse for this group that was all ready to race. This horse's name was *Caspari*, a son of *Big Towner*, out of a *Bret Hanover* mare. The horse looked perfectly okay, so we bought him for twelve thousand dollars. I called home with the news of this purchase and everyone was excited. The golfing group would make tons of money that would finance golfing trips for years to come.

We arrived back at the farm at about two o'clock in the morning. For some reason I took several blood samples from *Caspari* before going home to bed.

The next morning when I returned to the farm I was in for a big surprise. *Caspari* was lying down in his stall. When I forced the horse to his feet, his knees were so painful that he couldn't stand for long and would lie back down.

We had been taken! *Caspari* showed absolutely no pain the day before the sale, but obviously had received large doses of pain killers to cover up the pain. I called the auction people who told me that I could present my complaint to an arbitration process, but unless I could prove the horse was drugged there would be little chance of canceling the sale.

Taking the blood samples the night before became my ace in the hole. I immediately sent a sample to the diagnostic lab at Cornell. The sample revealed huge amounts of Butazuliden, a potent pain killer. When I called the auction people they gave me a date for a hearing in front of an arbitrator.

With my lab reports in hand, Sam Vulcano (my son-in-law lawyer and one of the owners) and I drove to New Jersey for the hearing. The arbitrator would not cancel the sale, but he did lower the purchase price to six thousand, giving us a refund of six grand.

Caspari's bad knees would be a problem for the rest of his days. We did get him to the races with treatment and swimming, but he did not fulfill the golfers' dream. In 1993, he made twenty-five starts, two wins, four seconds, five thirds, and earnings of $7,489. In 1994, *Caspari* had twelve starts, one win, one second, no thirds, and earnings of $1,814. This was a horrendous losing proposition for the golfers. I decided to take ownership of the horse and cancel the training bill. They had lost one hundred percent of their investment.

I kept *Caspari* for the next two years. In 1996 he made five starts, one win, no seconds or thirds, and earnings of seven hundred dollars. During 1997 as a major depression consumed my energy and interest in treating *Caspari*, he made four starts, no firsts, seconds, or thirds, and earnings of sixty dollars. *Caspari's* racing career was over.

He left the farm together with the rest of my retired horses in the truck of a horse dealer. His final destination was unknown, but I fear it may have been the slaughter house. He was too lame for a buggy horse.

Caspari was a nice horse, but a victim of abuse as a two year old. The large purses for two-year-old races contribute to overtraining and injecting joints of young horses that are still growing. In his case, the cartilage in the knee joints was destroyed as a result of cortisone injections.

The racing of horses should not start until they are three years of age. This rule change would correct the abuse of other young horses like *Caspari*.

If you ever become interested in becoming an owner, remember this advice: *Buyer beware!*

APPENDIX

In 1992, the Post Standard in Syracuse, New York published the following:

TRAINER HAS HIS LIFE BACK IN HARNESS

■ With health problems behind him, Dr. Jim Marshall finds happiness on his horse farm.

By DONNIE WEBB
The Post-Standard

CHITTENANGO — Ruth Marshall should have been horrified. But when her husband finally was diagnosed with a brain tumor, she admits she was relieved.

It explained the depression, the sleepless nights. It explained the two suicide attempts. It explained what happened to her husband of 31 years, retired Fayetteville veterinarian Dr. Jim Marshall.

Doctors at the Mayo Clinic in Rochester, Minn., removed a benign tumor from Marshall's pituitary gland in January 1987. He says doctors believed the quarter-size tumor had been there for 10 to 15 years and had brought on the depression that all but destroyed his life.

Now, Marshall has taken his life by the reins. At 58, he has taken on a new career as a harness racing trainer.

He has built a sprawling operation on his 213-acre farm just outside Chittenango. The facility includes a five-eighths-mile track, a 50-by-250-foot training pond, numerous paddocks and ample romping room for the 25 horses who frolic in the scenic countryside.

Marshall also has a provisional driver's license at Vernon Downs. He won his first race in eight starts May 28 behind JMF's Misty, an 8-5 favorite who paced a personal-best time of 1:59.2. Marshall will be in the sulky again Sunday driving National Star, an 11-year-old horse that has great sentimental value.

Marshall bought a one-fifth share of National Star in 1984 and later sold his interest, but he bought the

(See TRAINER, Page C-3)

JIM COMMENTUCCI/The Post-Standard

Dr. Jim Marshall

■ **Age:** 58

■ **Family:** Ruth, his wife of 31 years; children, Otis, Peter, Cynthia and Jennifer.

■ **Residence:** Fayetteville

■ **Occupation:** Retired veterinarian and full-time harness racing owner, trainer and driver. He operates a 213-acre farm in Chittenango.

■ **First victory:** May 28 in the sixth race at Vernon Downs. Driving JMF's Misty, Marshall took the lead at the quarter-pole and won the mile race by four lengths in 1:59.2.

■ **In training:** In 34 starts at Vernon, Marshall's horses have five victories, one second and two thirds. They have won $7,718.

THE POST-STANDARD/Saturday, June 20, 1992/PAGE C-3

SPORTS

Trainer Gets Back On Track

Caspari exercises Friday by doing laps at Dr. Jim Marshall's farm in Chittenango. Marshall has his horses swim six to eight laps per workout in the 14-foot deep pond.

(TRAINER, from Page C-1)

horse again after regaining his health. "He's like an old friend," Marshall says.

Training and driving is an ambitious undertaking for any newcomer to the volatile horse business, but it is especially daunting given Marshall's medical history.

"He's come a long way," says trainer Chuck Connor, who rents barn space from Marshall. "He's got a good facility and a lot of great ideas on how to manage horses and keep them in their natural environment. He does pretty well."

Connor says he believes Marshall's farm probably is the only one in Central New York that combines a track, swimming pool and "turnout facility" for the horses. Marshall bought the property in 1984 with the idea of getting into the harness racing business after retiring from his veterinary practice, but it wasn't until he had his health scared away that the project came into focus.

Marshall says he feels rehabilitated and liberated from the dark days of his depression. The only reminders are a limp caused by a broken back — the result of an attempt to take his life — and the anti-depressant medication he must take every day.

Marshall moseys around the farm he lovingly calls his "Ponderosa" on either a golf cart or a four-wheel all-terrain vehicle. And he obviously feels good enough to take the reins of the horses he trains.

Ruth Marshall said the transformation in her husband has been remarkable. In essence, she has her husband back. Their son, Peter, who works the farm with his father, said the horse business has been therapeutic.

"It's done a lot of good for him," he says. "It's brought him a lot of happiness and success. There's a big difference in his outlook. It's brought more meaning to his life."

Jim Marshall does not train horses that belong to others. He shops around for horses that, as Connor puts it, "are one step away from the Amish." Marshall says that helps him keep his overhead low. And with his veterinary background and holistic approach to training, Marshall believes there is potential in every horse.

One of the unique aspects of his facility is the pond, which is fed by a natural spring. Horses are led into the 14-foot deep pond, where they swim laps depending on their conditioning. Marshall says it's an excellent method for improving the horses' cardiovascular conditioning. He also says the horses have fun.

And that seems to be his approach.

"It's a challenge, a mind game," Marshall says. "We try to keep the horses happy. And that's where we think we have an edge in training. Horses that get locked in a barn, they can get depressed."

The highlight of Marshall's brief second career was the night he drove JMF's Mixty to his first victory at Vernon. Connor, who was driving My Hi Fella N in the same race, says Marshall drove his horse boldly to the front and when he finished, "he let a big 'Yahoo!' out with the whip in the air."

Connor says he has heard some grumbling among fans and even a few drivers about Marshall's age.

"A lot of people don't think I should be out there because of my age," says Marshall, who will turn 59 in November. "But I'll be out there as long as my health allows. And also, I'm going to try and win."

And that's just fine with Ruth Marshall. Her husband is healthy and happy. He has abandoned retirement for a second career.

"Next to his children and grandchildren, this is probably the number one thing in his life," she says.

Jim Marshall has come full circle. He grew up on a farm in Munnsville, and he plans to spend the rest of his life on his farm in Chittenango.

There are more bad days than good in racing, but he says every day is one to savor.

"It was kind of a miracle," he says of his new lease on life. "I look at every day as a bonus.

"That night I won, when I was jogging back to the winner's circle, I thought about how far I came back . . . and I was grateful."

In August of 2003, *Harness Racing Communications* published the following:

═══════*HARNESS RACING*═══════
COMMUNICATIONS
41 Highway 34, Suite 20, Colts Neck, New Jersey 07722-1736 · Phone (732) 780-3700 · Fax (732) 780-2699 · E-Mail HRCNEWS@AOL.COM

| August 4, 2003 | HARNESS RACING COMMUNICATIONS | VOL. 13, NO. 25 |

RETIRED VET USES ANIMALS TO HELP PEOPLE

JMF'S Sam has won 46 races and $127,386 in his harness racing career, yet those numbers are fairly inconsequential to his owner, Dr. James Marshall. As the saying goes, you can't put a price on happiness. And on his off days, JMF'S Sam, an 11-year-old pacer, pulls a load much greater than sulky.

Dr. Marshall, a 69-year-old retired veterinarian from Fayetteville, New York, near Syracuse, suffered from depression for 23 years. During that time, he twice tried to commit suicide - once at his farm and once in Boston's Logan Airport. He had four hospital stays because of his condition. Eventually, doctors discovered a brain tumor and a sleep disorder that both were partially responsible for his depression. Both were successfully treated, and Dr. Marshall has been recovered for three years.

During his therapy, Dr. Marshall found peace and tranquility on the farm, and found the presence of the animals there to be helpful. He saw animals giving birth, and at that point he began to realize the gift of life. He promised himself that he would spread the word and help others when he recovered.

So last year Dr. Marshall created the Jim Marshall Farms Foundation Inc., and in May he started the "Walk and Talk" program. From 1 to 4 p.m. each Sunday through October, people are invited to "observe the miracle of life" for themselves in the puppies, foals, ducklings, lambs, and other animals on the 84-acre property. Dr. Marshall no longer owns the farm, which in 1999 he donated to ARISE Child and Family Service, a group that works with the disabled. The Jim Marshall Farms Foundation Inc. is an approved 501(c)(3) not-for-profit organization.

"These sessions aren't entertainment for the general public," Dr. Marshall said about his program. "Everyone is expected to be supportive of our mission, which is helping people feel better. The farm is a refuge from troubles and a place where you are greeted with a friendly smile, a kind word, and the unconditional love that animals can provide."

JMF'S Sam, who last raced August 2 at Vernon Downs, is one of those animals. He is one of the horses used to give carriage rides during the "Walk and Talk" sessions. Dr. Marshall and his son, James Jr., who is a farrier, have approximately 20 Standardbreds on the farm and three trotting mares in foal. All of the horses bred by Dr. Marshall, a 1957 graduate of Cornell University's vet program, are named for people who have been important to him. Sam, for example, is named after his son-in-law. JMF'S Alice, an unraced pacer, is being used by ARISE to pull wheelchair-bound people in a cart specially designed by Dr. Marshall.

Dr. Marshall's program isn't designed to provide therapy or clinical help, and all guests are advised to seek professional help for depression. All guests at the farm - whether volunteers or people seeking help - wear an identification tag that gives only their first names. There also are "Life Mentors," people who have had personal experience with depression in their own lives or in the lives of a loved one.

"We don't present them as experts," Dr. Marshall said. "Just good citizens that are willing to help others, Our program requires that all contact and communication with visitors occur at the farm facility."

In addition to coming up with the idea for the program, Dr. Marshall constructed 22 benches by hand and placed them at 100-yard intervals around the farm's "people track," not to be confused with the five-eighths of a mile training track Dr. Marshall built for his Standardbreds. His career as a Standardbred trainer has seen him work with Sister Gold - a nine-year-old pacing mare who was winless in 2000 and 2001, but won a whopping 25 races in 46 starts in 2002, along with $29,668.

While he admits that he and his son, "have a lot of fun with the farm," it's helping others battle depression that gives Dr. Marshall the most satisfaction.

"The most tragic occurrence that can happen in our lives is to lose a child, relative, or a friend to suicide," Dr. Marshall said. "This leaves us with a lifetime of wondering what we could have done to save this precious life. Our goal here is to rekindle happiness and the recognition of the gift of life that everyone should enjoy."

For more information about the program, or to make a donation, call Dr. Marshall at 315-687-5064.

The following are articles that were published in 2003 promoting the start of Jim Marshall Farms Foundation, Inc.:

Horse healing: non-profits help the disabled

by Alaina Potokus

At Jim Marshall Farms in Chittenango, animals are helping people learn an important life lesson: "When you help someone else, you help yourself."

By inviting depression patients out to the farm on Sunday afternoons from May until October for a relaxing "Walk and Talk," retired Fayetteville veterinarian Dr. Jim Marshall hopes to use his own personal experiences to help others overcome the illness that plagued him for nearly 23 years.

"The animals and the peace of the country is a whole lot more therapeutic than going to the 14th floor of the State Tower building," Marshall said. "Instead of going to psychiatrist and spending $150 a session, people struggling with depression can spend an afternoon with us on the farm for nothing."

Born and raised on a dairy farm in Minnsville, Marshall graduated from Cornell with a degree in veterinary medicine in 1957. Settling in Fayetteville in 1963, he founded the Fayetteville Veterinary Hospital where he would treat farm animals and companion pets for the next 30 years.

Marshall started to have problems with depressive illness in 1977 at age 43. As a result, he sold his veterinary practice in 1990. In 1999, he gifted 84 acres of his Chittenango farm to the not-for-profit organization ARISE for exclusive use of people with disabilities.

"I went through some real bad times," Marshall said. "I wanted something good to happen to the farm."

During his 23-year battle with depression, Marshall found comfort in the peace and tranquility of the farm environment where he had grown up. After recovering from the illness in 2000, he decided to form a foundation to assist those suffering from the disease that clouded so many years of his life.

"When I went through it, I never thought anyone recovered because there were no success stories," Marshall said. "I kind of vowed that if I ever did recover I would tell the world and my story to give hope to others."

The Jim Marshall Farms Foundation now shares space with "ARISE at the Farm," where Marshall encourages his visitors to observe the "miracle of life" in young puppies, foals and lambs. Horse-drawn carriage rides give an overview of the farm, while a "People Track" with benches positioned every 100 yards allows participants to enjoy

Jim Marshall, a retired veterinarian, formerly of Fayetteville, started a non-profit organization dedicated to helping people fighting depression.

the picturesque scenery.

"It's the only place in Central New York where you can rest every 100 yards, walk three-quarters of a mile and come back to where you started," Marshall said with a grin.

To encourage openness and allow for privacy, program participants wear badges and are identified only by their first names. Those singled out as "Life Mentors" are qualified volunteers who have had personal experience with depression and are willing to discuss specific problems with participants.

"They can take a walk or just sit on the benches and talk," said Linda, a life mentor with the program. "It's whatever everyone is most comfortable with."

In the upcoming months, Marshall hopes to erect several buildings on the farm that will enable him to hold meetings year-round. Although he doesn't profess to be a substitute for seeking professional help, Marshall said he hopes his program will be a "refuge from trouble where you are greeted by a friendly smile, a kind word and the unconditional love that animals can provide."

"Depression and depressive illness hangs on so long that I think people need a regular support program," Marshall said. "It's not like a broken bone that takes eight weeks to heal. It goes on for years. And we're here to help."

The Jim Marshall Farms Foundation provides support for those suffering from depressive illnesses every Sunday through October from 1 to 4 p.m. at ARISE at the Farm, New Boston Road, Chittenango. For more information, call 687-5064.

Syracuse Post Standard - July 13, 2003

Farm lets depressed people help others, and themselves

Syracuse Post Standard 7/30/0

By Amber Smith
Staff writer

KATHY DUNN, of Erieville, pets a horse at the Jim Marshall Farm Foundation in Chittenango. The farm holds a Walk & Talk program to help people with depression.

Laurie was on medication, coming out of her depression, on a hectic Sunday this spring. She raced from the house with her two daughters without feeding them, so they wouldn't be late for church. They stopped at the Hamlet Diner in Chittenango for a quick breakfast. That's where she saw a flier for "Doc's Walk & Talk."

"Come and join us in helping to fight depression," it read. "Visit with animals, take carriage rides, walk around the track and interact with various people. You'll feel great!"

She went that afternoon, and she did feel great. Now she makes regular visits with her husband and sons, too.

"It's serene. It's peaceful,"

she says. "If you ask me, it's God's medicine for us."

Wildflowers dot the pasture in clumps, and on this recent 85-degree day the fresh country air carries a hint of skunk. A train whistles in the distance, and swallows dart in and out of a barn, tending a nest. Windmills along Route 5 are visible, though tiny, from one of the 22 benches Dr. James Marshall made by hand and placed in 100-yard increments around the walking track.

This is his creation, his life, his way of giving back.

Marshall, a retired veterinarian from Fayetteville, tried to kill himself twice, during bouts of depression that spanned 23 years. He's been better the past three years, but he still takes

medication and plans to for the rest of his life.

"I promised my wife I always would," he says. "It's awful hard to live with someone who's depressed. She doesn't want to go back to those days."

He still derives serenity from being around the horses and the other farm animals. He says they're what saved him. In the autobiography he is writing, he says, "I talk about the many horses I've had as being my best therapists."

What's so special about animals?

"I would say their unconditional love," says Marshall. "Your pet is never going to tell you to snap out of it."

Marshall grew up on a dairy farm in Mexxeville and headed

ANIMALS, PAGE 6-2

Animals at farm offer reprieve from depression

ANIMALS, FROM PAGE 1-1

to Cornell University, intending to follow the family tradition of farming. He walked through the veterinary school one day, and that sparked his interest. He spoke to a guidance counselor about the possibility of attending the school.

"He said I'd taken all the wrong courses," Marshall recalls. In order to even be considered, he'd have to take tough classes like organic chemistry and advanced zoology all together the next semester. The advisor told him it couldn't be done, that he'd "bust out" trying.

"It made me so mad," Marshall says, feisty at the recollection. At midterm he had a 93 average. They accepted him into the school, thinking he was brainy. He had a strong background from working his family farm, but more than anything, Marshall was just determined.

He opened the Fayetteville Veterinary Hospital in 1962 and ran the practice until he sold it in 1990.

Marshall bought 84 acres of North Chittenango pasture land in 1984, so he'd have a place to pursue his hobby of harness racing. He built the main stable, a track and some other barns before giving the property to ARISE in 1999, for use with people with disabilities. Now ARISE lets him use the property on Sunday afternoons, and he hopes to work out a deal to build a chapel on the land.

His trouble with depression

begins when he was 43, and for 23 years he battled the disease. Only his family and close friends knew. He made two suicide attempts — one at the farm and one at Boston's Logan Airport — and had four hospital stays for depression. Eventually doctors discovered a brain tumor.

"They're (the animals) not judgmental. They don't talk back. They're not demanding."
— Laurie, visitor to Jim Marshall Farm

During one hospital stay, Marshall asked a minister whether he knew anyone who had recovered from the depths of a suicide attempt. The minister answered honestly: He didn't.

Like the brash college student who put the guidance counselor in his place, Marshall decided then that he would recover, and he would tell everyone about it.

That's what he's doing with the farm.

On any given Sunday, people take carriage rides around the track, walk along a paved path, stroll through the barns looking at the baby ducks, the lazing rabbits, the goats. They go by first

names only. Some are here as guests. Some are "life mentors," people who may have experience with depression but definitely have a desire to help others. It's hard to tell them apart.

On this recent Sunday, a woman named Kathy visits. She's struggled with a bipolar disorder since high school and tried to kill herself at the beginning of college. She walks to the edge of a corral for a while, pets the horses and gazes across the pasture, then returns to Marshall. They get to talking.

"Everybody thinks a pill is going to be the magic cure. I didn't find it that way," he tells her. Though Marshall still takes medication, he credits a breathing machine with allowing him a solid night's sleep and, therefore, curing his depression.

"I fought taking the medication because I didn't want to be a zombie," Kathy says, explaining that doctors still have her on a small dose of generic Prozac. "If I stop taking it, I notice.

"I do miss the high highs," she says, "but I can do without them if I don't get the low lows."

A woman named Martha arrives at the farm. She sees a psychiatrist for depression, though she says she's never contemplated suicide. She was drawn to the farm today because, as she explains, "I wanted to go somewhere and be with someone but not really be with anyone."

Laurie gets there later, her

husband and four kids and a nephew piling out of the van with her and quickly dispersing to check out the barns. Now that she's recovering from the tendency to be a do-it-all mom, Laurie says she looks forward to her time with the animals.

"They're not judgmental.

"Everybody thinks a pill is going to be the magic cure. I didn't find it that way."
— Jim Marshall, of Jim Marshall Farm Foundation

she says. "They don't talk back. They're not demanding."

One of the kids spots a frog, bleeding in the shade outside of the barn.

The wound appears grave, and someone wonders whether it would be more humane to finish the poor frog off.

Marshall scoops up the frog, a small puddle of blood accumulated on its head, and looks him over. "Nah, he'll live," proclaims the vet. "He needs some tall grass."

He carries the reptile to a sink and cleans the wound and pats it with a paper towel. Then he rides a golf cart to a spot in the pasture and lets the frog go.

Marshall lives his motto: When you help others, you help yourself.

DARD Sunday, April 20, 2003

COMMUNITY

DR. JIM MARSHALL, a retired veterinarian who suffered for many years from depression, is beginning a nonprofit organization to provide an informal mental health therapy through animals at a farm that he shares with ARISE. He is shown with Big Ben The Blonde Belgian. The farm is on New Boston Road in North Chittenango.

Tapping Animal Spirits

Farm setting to become available to depression sufferers

By Frank Brieaddy
Staff writer

A retired Fayetteville veterinarian who battled depression for 23 years believes that being around animals and helping other people were two of the most important elements of his recovery.

Dr. Jim Marshall has launched a nonprofit group that soon will welcome people suffering from depression to a North Chittenango farm setting, where they can enjoy an uplifting visit with horses, puppies and a variety of barnyard animals while sharing support with others.

"The secret to getting out of depression is helping someone else," he said. "We want to get them away from being a patient all the time, and, 'Woe is me.'"

The Jim Marshall Farms Foundation will begin welcoming people touched by depression and those willing to support them from 1 to 4 p.m. May 4 and every Sunday thereafter through October at ARISE at the Farm, New Boston Road.

Marshall donated the 84-acre farm to ARISE Child and Family Service in 2000 and has arranged to use it in the spring, summer and fall for his new project.

The program is not intended to provide clinical help or even therapy, but rather to share support among the clients and volunteers. Everyone will be advised to seek professional help for depression.

Activities will be unstructured. There

Jim Marshall Farms Foundation

What: A nonprofit group offering people suffering from depression support in a farm setting.

Where: ARISE at the Farm, New Boston Road, North Chittenango.

How to help: The foundation is a public charity registered with the Internal Revenue Service. Jim Marshall can be reached by mail at 1927 New Boston Road, Chittenango 13037, or by phone at 687-5064.

will be carriage rides, opportunities to pet the animals and quiet places where visitors can share their concerns or offer support to others. Marshall calls it a "walk and talk."

Marshall, 69, is quick to note that his expertise comes only from his own recovery, which wasn't complete until about three years ago. "I only know what my own experience was."

Those seeking support and volunteers offering to help will be indistinguishable at the farm. All will wear an identification tag with just their first names. Marshall is designating a few trusted volunteers — generally retired people he finds to be extra helpful — as "life mentors." They'll be identified.

The veterinarian said he will soon be contacting all of the psychiatrists in the Central New York area to talk to them about his program.

Born in Munnsville, Marshall had a successful veterinary practice before he started to suffer from depression at age 43 in 1977. He tried to commit suicide at the farm in 1983 and again at Boston's Logan Airport, when he was en route to one of four separate hospital placements.

"It was a very bad time in my life," Marshall said.

Doctors eventually found he had both a sleep disorder and a brain tumor (both successfully treated), which were partially responsible for his depression.

During his last hospital stay, Marshall said, he would routinely walk an older woman in a wheelchair through a park-like setting. Helping her helped him greatly, he said.

His own therapy at the farm included the sight of animals giving birth. He said it made him appreciate the gift of life, which people with depression often underestimate.

Marshall is negotiating with ARISE to buy back seven vacant acres at the farm, where he would like to construct a multipurpose building and a chapel to house his nonprofit organization.

Right now, the Jim Marshall Farms Foundation is operating on Marshall's labor with two employees and financial support from close friends.

In Good Health — Nov 2003 issue #47

Mental health: Walk and Talk helps alleviate depression

A Fayetteville vet started program after several depression crises that led to two suicide attempts

By Connie Hannon

For almost 40 years, James O. Marshall, DVM, was a successful professional, family man and community leader running the Fayetteville Veterinarian Hospital in Syracuse, a modern suburb, a practice he literally and figuratively built from the ground up. He also suffered from severe clinical depression for 15 years during that time—and 10 years after selling the practice in 1998—that included two suicide attempts.

Convinced he has finally reclaimed his life, his message is one of hope, something he last wrote in 1985. And through the Jim Marshall Farms Foundation he hopes to help others suffering from depressive illness from ever slitting to the depth he did.

The first stage of Marshall's mission has been taking place on Sundays—dubbed the Walk & Talk Program—in an informal and non-clinical setting, on farmland in Chittenango that attracted his ARISE services ago. Since May, people suffering from, or those concerned about clinical depression have gathered there for varying reasons, whether it's talking to others, taking horse and buggy rides, feeding or petting the farm animals and horses or just walking around in the fresh air.

Raised on a Madison County farm, Marshall believes the simple, outdoor setting is therapeutic, especially the animals.

"Animals give unconditional love and that often can be just the lift needed at times," he says. After selling his veterinarian practice, breeding and racing horses on the inviting stream. He owns 150 acres adjacent to the farmland he donated.

The walk-and-talks are designed to help others realize that they are not alone and there is hope of recovery from depressive illness. The theme of the program is "where animals help people" and the motto is "when you help someone, you help yourself." There Farms Foundation, a not-for-profit organization, to help fund the next two stages of the mission.

Establishing the non-profit foundation was essential. "Depression is such a wide-ranging illness that I knew I could never accomplish my goals with just my resources," he says. While the Sunday meetings at the farm will be scaled back to once a month during the winter, Marshall is turning his attention to phase two, a multi-purpose professional building, to complement the Walk & Talk Program, that will include a health component. A third element, an out-door national chapel, is also planned.

"Having attempted suicide twice while depths and secretive nature of depressive illness," Marshall says. "Consequently, I hope my story and the eventual development of

the farm into a viable therapeutic destination will be an inspiration to others suffering from the disease, whether they are young people, homemakers, successful business people or people that have fought for so long that they are losing hope."

Here are a few things to help put depression in perspective. In its October report, a blue-ribbon government task force studying national gun violence reported 10,801 gun-related deaths during 2001. That may or may not be striking. But this is: According to the report, there were almost 6,000 more gun-related suicides—a total of 16,586—that year.

Closer to home, there is this mindshaking nature of the illness. Marshall tried to take up deer hunting during the '90s. He built a deer tree-stand and studied the habits of deer before hunting season started. Then, perched and rifle in hand, he took aim at a legal deer walking with her growing fawns. He couldn't shoot, though, as he thought of the young deer a mass their parent. Yet while he could not shoot an animal, depressive illness caused him to turn a gun on himself in 1985. Even with eight years of professional therapy, he rationalized recovery was hopeless and suicide was the best option for himself and his family. The second attempt happened two weeks later.

Marshall stresses that the walk-and-talks are meant for support and are not professional therapy. Individuals at the farm are encour-

Jim Marshall holds Big Ben, one of Jim Marshall Farms' animals that he hopes can help people deal with depressive illness. Since May those people and concerned volunteers have been meeting on Sundays in an informal setting in Chittenango.

aged to contact mental health professionals of their choosing and follow their directions. Marshall was under psychiatric care from 1977 to 2000 and is convinced something like this laid-back program on the farm might have complemented formal treatment, even preventing him from bottoming out.

"For 25 years I was on a depressive roller coaster, but the suicidal period when I decided to end my life lasted only a few months." Marshall says. "I realize how difficult it is for others to understand how a person can reach that point, but that's the grip this illness had on me.

"It is also the reason Marshall is dedicated to provide the support, camaraderie and caring workers don't breach those depths. There is nothing that I can think of worse than losing a friend or relative to suicide," he says.

For more information on the Jim Marshall Farms Foundation and the Walk and Talk Program, call 315-687-5464.

In February 2004, I shared my manuscript with a mental health professional, who in turn shared it with one of his patients. The patient suffered severe depression for years and has survived one suicide attempt.

When she finished the book she wrote me the following letter that warmed my heart and helped me realize that my effort was worthwhile.

March 9, 2004

Dear Doc:

I wanted to take this opportunity to inform you how much I enjoyed reading your book *Where Animals Help People*.

Once I started to read it, I couldn't put it down! (It took me less than four hours to read it.) I think being able to relate so much to what you wrote about made it impossible for me to stop.

I found it very interesting to read about your childhood on the family farm and the closeness you felt to your extended family. The mixture of your quirky tales about your practice blended well with the story of your struggle with depression. I think it's well balanced so people that haven't had to deal with mental illness won't be overwhelmed by the dark words you used to describe your suicide attempts and your prolonged suffering. I think that that's important because you want to reach many different people with your book. Both people that have struggled with depression and those that haven't...you know...the "lucky" ones.

The Friday afternoon that I read your book started as a day filled with angst. But I realized the more pages that I turned the more I was being helped. About half way through I opened the blinds in my bedroom and I sat on my bed and let the sun warm my body as I continued to read. To a "normal" person that wouldn't have much meaning, but to me it was a big deal. As you know, the days that are the darkest in our lives we tend to isolate and draw inward. So there aren't many days that I let the sunshine in. Opening the blinds that afternoon was a BIG deal for me.

Your vision for The Farm is well stated also. Your words give readers a clear picture why you started your foundation and why you hope it continues to prosper. As I read about all the horses you've trained and rehabilitated over the past few years it made me want to hop in my car and venture down to your barn. My depression and anxiety is helped so much by your foundation. It's simple...it's the animals; they draw me in just like a fly to fly-paper.

Your book will be read and absorbed by so many people that need to be helped. They'll be able to relate to your illness and know that there's hope. They'll be able to see that those of us that suffer from this disease can have a future without pain. We don't have to die to overcome our emotions. We can get better; you've shown us that with your courageous words of wisdom and hope.

I thank God that your attempts to end your life failed. I believe it was fate. You have a gift of writing and reaching out to those in need. This is your purpose in life: to get the word

out to the millions who suffer from depression and need to be helped. You my friend are a blessing.

I can't wait until your book is published so that I'm able to share it with my family and friends. My hope is that they'll be touched by its content and learn more about what it's like to live with depression and a taste for death.

Best of luck with your book. I look forward to seeing you soon.

0-595-31971-8

Printed in the United States
24941LVS00006B/133-150